GETTING COMPUTER JOBS ABROAD

Michael Powell

ComputerWeekly

Published by:

Computer Weekly Publications
Quadrant House
Sutton
Surrey
SM2 5AS

Publications Manager: John Riley
Deputy Publications Manager: Robin Frampton
Publications Executive: Katherine Canham

REED
BUSINESS
PUBLISHING

© 1991

Reprinted 1991

A catalogue record for this book is available from the British Library

ISBN 1-85384-016-5

Printed by Hobbs The Printers, Southampton

CONTENTS

PREFACE

Michael Powell's successful book *Considering Computer Contracting?* has helped many computer professionals break loose from being a full-time employee, often dramatically increasing their income in the process. The book is now in its second edition and continues to be in great demand. Now, Michael Powell has turned his attention to opportunities overseas for computer professionals, whether as full-time employees or as contractors.

With widening European markets and easier worldwide communications, the opportunities for taking computer skills abroad have increased in some areas. Recent events, however, have turned the Middle East into a less likely destination. North America is still a popular destination, since language is not a problem (except in French Canada), and the standard of living is high.

This book explains how to take the first step towards working abroad. The author gives general data on the computer scene, major industries and the economy in each country is considered. Information is given about job opportunities, whether languages are required, work permits, cost of living, taxation, housing, transport, etc.

The author also covers work opportunities for partners, and other matters which could affect their decision to join you, or bring children to live in the country, such as healthcare, political stability, attitudes to women, and educational possibilities. A list of Embassies and Computing Services Associations will help you gather up additional information of relevance to your own particular situation.

Whatever the reason for wanting to work abroad - this book will help you plan your next move.

THE AUTHOR

Michael Powell has worked in the computer industry since leaving Oxford University in 1970. After some years working his way through programming and systems analysis jobs, he became a contractor in 1975, before returning to full-time employment in the software industry. He moved into sales and reached the position of European Marketing Manager with Pansophic Systems. For some years, he ran his own software products business, modifying and writing business accounting systems. He returned to contracting in 1984 and has been working as a freelance consultant since then.

He combines contracting with freelance writing in the computer and daily press. However, his real love is opera singing and contracting provides him with the right environment to enjoy this. He is a semi-professional tenor who took a tenor lead in Britten's *Rape of Lucretia* at the 1987 Aldeburgh Festival.

Michael Powell is married with two children.

CHAPTER 1

OVERVIEW

The world is becoming ever smaller. It does not seem very long ago that the concept of air travel to far off places was romantic and smacked of great riches. Now it is extremely unusual to find a person without a passport.

You used to have to join the forces or the diplomatic corps to work abroad. Now, the world is your oyster. Especially in the burgeoning data processing industry, there are opportunities almost everywhere. However if, like Fred Astaire, you expect to see the world, what you will actually see is the central processing unit (CPU).

THE CHANGING WORLD SITUATION

Since this book was originally planned two years ago, the world has changed radically. At that time, we did not intend to cover 'iron curtain' countries, for obvious reasons. Although Glasnost was being talked about, it was still treated with suspicion by most of us. East Germany has now ceased to exist. The new Germany is the largest unit in Europe. However, its powerful economy will be under strain for some time as it absorbs the costs of modernising clapped-out East German industry.

Two years ago, the best gravy train of all to ride was in the Middle East - although it was not quite as attractive as it had been. A long section had been prepared on the area, and Kuwait had been listed as the country offering most openings after Saudi Arabia. Although we had not prepared so much data about Iraq, it was on the list with a certain amount of data collected.

All that has had to change. Sadly, because of the efforts of one man, the Middle East is again in a similar state of turmoil to that which it has historically suffered. It would be unwise to recommend anyone to consider working over there (save, perhaps as a supplier to the US armed forces) until the dust of the desert has settled. With Kuwait free from Iraq occupation again, many new opportunities are possible there as the country sets about rebuilding.

On the other hand, the one-time Eastern Bloc countries are now becoming more open and will be crying out for western expertise to help modernise their industries and enable them to build viable systems of government and commerce. The opportunities are still shrouded in the polluted miasma of planned economies, and they are desperately short of hard currency. However, the opportunities must be there.

THE FORMAT OF THE BOOK

This book is intended to provide some guidelines for DP personnel contemplating working overseas on contract and as permanent staff. Contracting will be the only option for some people in some countries which limit the influx of permanent residents in a number of ways.

We have investigated the work permit situation in the countries covered, and tried to give a flavour of the hoops through which you may be expected to jump to be allowed in.

The format of the book is a country by country analysis of the main countries in which job opportunities exist for DP staff - or in which computer staff would like to find opportunities. The country summaries contain information which has been gleaned from a variety of sources.

Some of this information may not be of obvious value to anyone looking for a job - what is the point, for example, of knowing the population, area or history of a country? The intention is to look behind the country and explain why it has the marketplace for skills which it has or has not got, and to give some idea of the way in which it has developed.

It is obvious that there are not opportunities for our sort of work in every country in the world. Therefore I have tried to identify the countries where there will be a number of opportunities. Even so, some of these offer little scope for expatriate workers, and are included because they might appear attractive in principle (because of climate, for instance).

It is certain that I will have rejected some countries where opportunities do occasionally exist. However, it would be unrealistic to include everywhere in the list. For example, I have not included the South American countries due to the problems of taking cash out of these countries and also due to the general lack of opportunities. Similiarly, India has not been included because its large indigenous population mean that opportunities are very rare. Some African countries do have sporadic jobs for DP staff on specific projects. However, these are not a regular feature and can be discounted in a general work of this type.

Choosing a Country to Work in

Choosing a country to live and work in is not a simple task. A job may look very attractive, but the social or political geography of the country may not be nearly so attractive. Many of the European countries, for instance, are reasonably familiar to us, in principle. However some background information should help you to make a rational choice by bringing your attention to something which you may not be aware of from the literature provided by embassies and consulates (*see* Appendices I and II).

Exchange Rates

Included in each section is a guide for the exchange rate in the country concerned, and the price of the largest cost which you are likely to incur - accommodation, wherever it is feasible to give such a figure. However, shortly before completion of the text, the Chancellor of the Exchequer announced that the pound would join the Exchange Rate Mechanism. This changed its value immediately, and the rates listed reflect that change. Although ERM membership is heralded as a neat way to control inflation by pegging the pound to other European currencies, it is not exactly clear what effect this change will have on overall exchange rates. Iraq's invasion of Kuwait in August 1990 - which sent the pound up because of its status as a petro-currency - and this ERM change have made all values rather suspect. (The intention is to keep the pound within six per cent of DM2.95). This kind of volatility is somewhat abnormal - but indicates that the value of foreign earnings can rise and fall very swiftly.

Opportunities for your Family

There is also a short section covering the sorts of opportunities which might exist outside your industry, and of the educational possibilities. If you are intending to move your family with you, it is important to know what opportunities may or may not exist for them locally, and what other expatriates do.

Checking on Permits

The information on work and residency permits is correct at the time of research. However, these matters change as the political and economic climate of the country changes. Therefore it is vital that you check with the consulate of the country before making detailed plans or burning your boats. It is not unknown for employees to resign, sell up and move into a country before they find that they are not entitled actually to work there. The result can be quite catastrophic, since you may be forced to return home 'sans job sans everything'.

Healthcare

It is also important to look carefully at such things as the local arrangements for healthcare. Things change, and the same advice applies - ask the consulate. To this end, I have included a sample questionnaire to give to the consulate of the country of your choice.

In practice, making them answer this may not be all that easy - in researching this book I have found that many of them will not answer written questions, preferring to deal with you face-to-face. A list of consular addresses can be found in Appendix II.

Wide Choice of Countries

In looking for a place to work overseas, the British citizen has a wide choice available. Apart from the obvious EC countries, attractive because of their proximity, there are many English speaking countries. Of these the old 'white' colonies, Canada, Australia, New Zealand and South Africa, probably offer the most choices, and the most open door.

If it is just money alone you are after, the Middle East has traditionally always been the place to go although recently salaries have not been so high, but the earlier caveat on travelling to those countries must apply.

Feedback

I happily acknowledge that this book, in its first edition, is unlikely to be as complete as the subject deserves. The research effort which went into its creation was as complete as it could be, but I was constrained by the availability of information, and time. I hope that the book can be updated by real live information - both as a result of changes which have occurred and because of errors and omissions in the original text.

Please contact the publisher if you have changes or suggestions to make about the form and content of *Getting Computer Jobs Abroad*, so that we can keep the book updated and improve it for you.

We open all the right doors for all the right people...

...in all the right places.

- Software '92 plc was formed in 1989 to provide specialist DP support and project management services to multinational corporations in the Single European market.

- During the past two years, we have enjoyed tremendous growth and are currently working with over 40 blue-chip clients in 7 European countries.

- We would like you to share in our success and are currently recruiting professional computer consultants.

- For future client projects we are interested in speaking to all computer professionals seeking opportunities on the continent. Through our offices in France and Germany we provide specialist and comprehensive support with a friendly and personal service. So let the experts arrange your passport to Europe.

- Contact us today:

    **Software '92 plc, 7 Trinity Place,
    Midland Drive, Sutton Coldfield, B72 1TX.
    Tel: 021-354 9911. Fax: 021-354 1565.**

software
'92 plc

FRANKFURT · PARIS · BIRMINGHAM · LONDON

CHAPTER 2

WORKING IN EUROPE

The largest overall economic unit in the world is Europe. Although this is not organised into a single unit, the combined economies have enormous purchasing power.

Europe is the cradle of western civilisation. From its shores went the colonists who created the great democracies of north America, as well as the sometimes more unstable regimes of middle and south America. If Europeans had not gone to Africa and Australia, those immense continents would be quite different (perhaps better, perhaps worse, who can say?).

The European wars of the twentieth century - the most destructive of all time - contributed to some of the greatest advances in science and industry. That may be an unpopular view, but if the Second World War had not happened, the computer might not yet have been made. It was advances in meteorology, code-breaking and radio which brought about the need for automatic computers, and the capability to build them. Now we can see a revival of Europe, following the end of the iron curtain - a leftover from that appalling war.

Europe for our purposes covers the landmass of most of the European Community (EC) - Belgium, France, Germany, Greece, Holland, Italy, Portugal, Spain and the United Kingdom. Also included is Switzerland and Austria - although not EC countries themselves, they lie between others which are, and offer some opportunities. Denmark - although part of the EC - is covered in the section on Scandinavia.

It is likely that the collapse of communism will make Europe an even more important unit in the future. Already politicians are looking forward to bringing Czechoslovakia, Poland and Yugoslavia into the EC, and perhaps even some of the socialist republics like Latvia, Lithuania and Estonia.

The problems which have arisen because of the collapse of the Russian empire will be felt for many years to come. The technological hole left by communism is enormous. Apart from the well-publicised need to clean up the industries even of relatively advanced countries, like East Germany (now absorbed into the Federal Republic), there will be a need to modernise the whole infrastructure of these countries. Poland today has a huge economic problem, and the jury is still out on how it will be solved.

The opportunities for expatriate workers in Europe are mainly constrained by language, which is also the missing cement in the binding together of the continent. Although English is very widely used, particularly in business, a knowledge of the local language can be important in day-to-day work. If you do not have the language, it may only be practical to work for a British or American subsidiary. However, this is by no means limiting in the major European countries, and may provide a stepping stone to a more indigenous life once the language has been mastered.

The presence of the EC is one of the main factors in creating mobility of labour from Britain. While many countries, such as Australia and the USA, are trying to reduce immigration, the EC countries have all agreed that, from an employment viewpoint, their borders should be open to all EC citizens.

In 1992 the barriers to trade between the twelve countries come down. In practice, however, there are sometimes problems because of residential qualifications - despite the good intentions of the bureaucrats. However, if the EC can get its act together, Europe will be a very good place to live in the twenty-first century.

FRANCE

Introduction

France is a country which defies all attempts at conformity. It has its own indigenous computer industry, uses different television standards, insists on the use of its own language, and remains proud of its heritage. Long may it continue.

1989 was the 200th anniversary of the French Revolution, and France remains the central pillar of Europe. Its population is similar to that of the UK, but its land area is far bigger - more than one third of the whole area occupied by all the EC countries. It is the largest European country by area. It is one of the world's leading industrial and agricultural powers - 20 per cent of its exports are agricultural. It is currently the world's fifth largest exporter.

France has a political system which dates from this revolution. There have been a number of periods since that time. Pre-revolutionary France is referred to as the Ancien Regime. Following that came the First Empire, ruled over by Napoleon. In 1814, the monarchy was briefly restored, until the last king of France abdicated in 1848, to make way for the Second Republic. In 1852, Louis Napoleon became emperor of the Second Empire. This lasted until 1870, when the Third Republic started. This was broken in 1940 when Germany invaded France, and established the Vichy government. The Fourth Republic was set up in 1946, but ended in 1958 at the time of the Algerian crisis. The present, Fifth Republic, was established then.

The French Government is headed by a President (currently M. Mitterand), who is more than a titular head, having actual executive power. He is elected for a seven year term. There is also a two chamber parliament to execute legislation. The current Prime Minister, Michel Rocard, was elected in 1988.

French business is far more independent than that of other European countries, apart perhaps from Britain. It is able to be self-sufficient in almost everything apart from oil. However, by an aggressive policy of nuclear power generation, it is able to satisfy most of its energy requirements.

Opportunities in the Computer Industry

Opportunities abound for computing staff in France, particularly those with good French. The marketplace is 1.5 times that of the UK, and the French have eagerly adopted all the latest equipment and standards.

Although France claims to have an independent, indigenous native computer industry, it is still heavily penetrated by IBM. In addition, Bull (which was Honeywell) is a thriving operation, and skills on that machinery are in demand. Like most of the world, Unix skills are becoming important, as are skills in all of open systems and C. France also boasts some of the largest European service companies, and has bought into the British services marketplace. Communications skills are keenly sought after and gain the highest salaries.

It is also worth noting that in much French computer job advertising the salary is not mentioned as the French belief is that you should primarily want to work for the company rather than just for the highest salary that you can find.

Language(s) Spoken

Of course, to work in France you need French. Even if you work for a British or American multinational, you will still need to speak some French. The word 'chauvinism' is itself French, and they expect you to fit in with them.

Actually, there are some companies whose main working language is English, and that is the second language in the country, but expect problems if you have no French at all.

French computerese is different from that in most countries. Whereas, in many languages, the American English terms are used instead of a translation, in France there are French words for almost everything. There are, for instance, three words for 'system' - 'systeme' means system in general, 'gestion' means an administrative or management system and 'logiciel' means a computer system. It is important to know the correct terms to do a computer job in French in France.

Currency

The French Franc currently stands at FrF9.92 to the pound.

Cost of Living

France covers such a large area, from the cold north coast to the balmy south, and has so many population centres that it is hard to generalise about costs.

Paris is a very expensive city to live, even compared to London. Some things (such as the underground railway, the Metro) are relatively cheap, but accommodation, food and goods are more expensive than at home.

Away from Paris, things are not so bad. Food is not too expensive, meals in restaurants are generally cheaper than their equivalent in the UK, and alcohol, particularly wine, is far cheaper.

Local Taxation

French income tax is low, but social security payments are very high. The taxation system is extremely complex, and best dealt with by an experienced French accountant. VAT is on multi-levels, between 15 and 33 per cent, depending upon the item being purchased. Take home pay in France is almost as low as anywhere in Europe.

Housing

Few people buy houses or apartments in Paris, it is much more normal to rent. You pay for the district - and there are some very expensive districts. French city dwellers do not normally live in houses, but in apartments. The cost of an unfurnished flat in Paris is about FrF9000 per month, and this figure is increasing. Outside the city prices are lower, and Paris has sprawling suburbs, with reasonable public transport.

Other Job Opportunities

As long as you speak the language, there are plenty of jobs to be found in France. However, a secretary qualified in English, with a smattering of French, may find it difficult to find employment. However, there are a number of multinationals in Paris which work in English and employ English staff.

Work Permits

Although a British passport does guarantee a 'right of abode' in France, assuming that the holder is described as a 'British Citizen', a residence permit is required should you want to live there. This will normally be granted if you have a job already arranged.

Educational Requirements

There are no specific academic requirements, since EC membership implies free movement of labour. However, qualifications or experience are naturally more in demand within the job marketplace.

The French are particularly keen on academic qualifications in the appropriate areas even more so than experience.

Major Urban Centres

France is very much centred around Paris, which numbers, including the suburbs, ten million people. This is on a par with Greater London.

The other major cities are Lyons and Marseilles - with around one million inhabitants apiece - Bordeaux, Lille, Nice, Toulouse and Strasbourg. This last city, although relatively small, occupies a prominent position as the second capital of the EC. As a result, there are many jobs there for multilingual personnel.

Major Industries

As befits its size, there is little that France does not produce. It is well supplied with natural resources, has considerable industrial expertise, and a well-educated workforce.

It has one of the most developed nuclear industries in the world (to offset the lack of oil), and is the European leader in the space and aerospace industries. French banking and commerce is also well-developed, although not as much so as Britain's.

Although France is often quoted as having the largest farming economy in the EC, the number of people employed on the land is dropping steadily. However, farming still represents an enormously important part of the French scene. Most of this is based around small family holdings for which, critics have said, the whole EC farm policy was designed.

Economic Prospects

France is a mature economy which has experienced prodigious growth since the shambles of the Second World War. It suffers the same problems of unemployment experienced throughout the world, although its inflation rate is lower than Britain's. Its growth in recent years has continued. The unemployment situation has forced the French government to restrict immigrants recently.

Educational System

French schooling is of very high quality, and demands high standards from pupils. Many expatriates are happy to let their children attend a French school. There are some English and American schools in Paris, and it is quite feasible to have children board in the UK - the air journey from London to Paris takes only one hour, and there are several flights per day.

Travel

The French are said to be some of the worst drivers in Europe. Their road system is excellent, apart from the roads around Paris, which are as congested as their equivalents in London.

A British driving licence is acceptable for two years, after which a French one is necessary.

If you are centred in Paris, and living close to public transport, you can manage without a car. However, as in England, the further you are from the centre the more important it becomes to have wheels. Parking in Paris is very difficult and best avoided if possible.

France is a very large country. Travel from the top to the bottom of the country takes many hours, even on the autoroutes. There are tolls on many of these roads, which can come as a shock to the unsuspecting. The speed limit is 130 kilometres per hour (about 81 miles per hour).

French railways are well subsidised and efficient, fares compare with those in the UK, but express services are very much faster. As you would expect, meals on French trains are far better than on British Rail.

The country is so large that air travel becomes a very viable alternative to road or rail, and there are airports in most major cities.

FEDERAL REPUBLIC OF GERMANY

Introduction

Germany is the most prosperous and populous country in the EC (now with 81 million inhabitants), as well as enjoying a reputation for engineering quality and efficiency which is thoroughly enviable.

The Federal Republic of Germany dates from 1949, when it was established by the victorious allies out of the ashes of the Third Reich. The origins of that conflict went back to the complex set of events which led to the First World War. In defeat (or surrender, Hitler and many other Germans would not accept the concept of defeat), Germany was turned, in 1918, into a democratic state. However, because of reparations to the victors, and the severe depression which followed, Hitler was able to gain power in the 1930s. In 1933 his Third Reich became the new Germany. Flaunting arms control agreements, he rebuilt the German forces, and started nibbling away at the countries around him, annexing the Rhineland, Austria and Czechoslovakia, before his invasion of Poland started the Second World War. The outcome of that is well-known. Germany was all but destroyed.

For years afterwards it was ruled by military men from the allies - France, Britain, the USA and Russia. Huge companies, like Volkswagen, owe their existence today to individual army officers who refused to let them be broken up, and set them on their way again. The country now has one of the strongest economies in the world - and once it has assimilated East Germany will be the dominant European superpower. Its output is largely industrial - agriculture plays only a minor role. Its success has enabled it to achieve one of the world's highest living standards.

A border was set up, and a new state, the German Democratic Republic - really just a Russian satellite - was created. This country, although for years the pride of the communist parties, was a failure. Its plant and machinery were outdated, it created monstrous pollution, and its peoples were condemned to a far lower standard of living than their prosperous West German neighbours. That legacy is still to be cleared up now that the two nations are re-united.

The German government is a parliamentary democracy with two chambers (the Bundesrat and Bundestag). These have been expanded to include members from East Germany. The leader of the government is the Chancellor - currently Helmut Kohl - and a titular president is the head of state. The country is divided into states, each of which has limited powers to enforce laws.

The Germans are a proud, hard-working people who have achieved success from within the depths of defeat. It is not geographically large, being now slightly over half the size of France.

In 1989 and 1990, Germany has seen the most profound changes. As the communist bloc buffer countries, Poland, Hungary and Czechoslovakia, turned against their masters, East Germany looked as if it would remain solidly communist. The flood of East German refugees, in their 1950s-style Trabant cars, pouring across the Czechoslovakian border into West Germany after 'holidays' in Czechoslavakia, became a temporary signal of the turmoil at home. In Christmas 1989 we were able to view those wonderfully emotive moments as the greatest symbol of post-war dictatorial tyranny, the Berlin Wall, came tumbling down. The full union of the two countries is now complete - or more precisely the absorption of East Germany by West.

So the Germans are happily past the shame of war and defeat, and able to hold their heads up high as one of the leading partners in the EC. There is no doubt that they will become an even greater force to be reckoned with when they have re-built East German industry, but for the time being they have the huge internal problem of rising unemployment (as inefficient factories close).

How this will affect opportunities for foreigners is not clear. There will still be openings for skilled staff, without doubt and the East German workforce have not yet got the technical training to fill the gaps. However, once they have learnt the necessary skills, the extra 17 million people will constitute a large labour pool, which will inevitably weave its way into all the different industries.

Opportunities in the Computer Industry

It used to be said that if all the English systems programmers went home the whole German DP industry would grind to a halt. Whether or not this is true, there are many opportunities, even if you have no German.

The German computer market is twice the size of Britain's - the largest in Europe. Because of the number of major cities, the available work is well spread - the type of work depending upon the local industrial scene.

Germany has an indigenous computer manufacturer, Siemens. However, their products are largely IBM compatible. IBM has a very strong presence, and IBM skills, particularly systems programming, are heavily in demand. There is also a strong DEC presence - indeed most of the manufacturers are represented in Germany in similar proportions to the UK.

Germans use English language products reasonably happily. Many technical manuals are in English, although there are translations available for some. German programmers are quite used to reading English. However, as in most other countries, users will not be so likely to speak English. Analyst jobs, therefore, will probably require a good knowledge of German. What is more, even a programmer may find that the manuals available are only in German.

Language(s) Spoken

The German language is not particularly easy to master, as it has a complex grammar. However it is very logical, with few of the irregularities which plague English or French. Many Germans speak English, and that is the second language. Although not desirable, it is possible to live and work in Germany without any German.

Currency

The deutschmark stood at DM2.87 to the pound in February 1991. It has been as low as DM4 to the pound, but regained strength in 1987 and 1988.

The level of the deutschmark is a cause for concern in Germany, which depends very much on trade with the rest of the world. German union has also had an adverse effect. The German government tied the, more or less worthless, ostmark to the deutschmark before union, as well as paying huge sums to the Soviet Union to help them re-patriate their army. This has not yet affected the currency value - so strong is the economy. It is difficult to see how the new Germany can fail not to become even more prosperous.

Cost of Living

Germany's cost of living is among the highest in Europe. However, its standard of living is commensurately high. As with most countries, alcohol and tobacco are cheaper than in the UK. Most other food items are not. Durables generally are cheaper - notably cars, which can be very much cheaper than their equivalents in the UK. For this reason, 'Yuppie' cars like BMWs and Porsches are more common in Germany.

Management salaries are often twice as high as in Britain. However secretarial and clerical wages are similar.

Local Taxation

Income tax is scaled according to earnings, up to a high rate of 56 per cent. VAT (MWT) is currently at 14 per cent.

Housing

Housing prices in Germany vary according to area. As in France, Germans in cities live in apartments rather than houses. In an average city, a three-bedroomed apartment is likely to cost around DM1800 per month.

Other Job Opportunities

There are many foreign nationals working in Germany, and they are not as discouraged as they are in other EC countries. Although German unemployment is rising, it is still lower than elsewhere in the world. However, the new East German labour pool will have an, as yet, unclear effect. There are also many companies whose main language is English-based in Germany.

Work Permits

A residence permit is required but not a work permit. This can be obtained from customs authorities - unless you can show that you have a job arranged, one may be withheld. British and EC citizens have freedom of entry and movement.

Educational Requirements

The same comments apply as with other EC countries.

Major Urban Centres

The largest city is Berlin, which was geographically separated from the rest of the country during the iron curtain years. Its inhabitants could only travel by road, rail and air links to the rest of the country.

The capital is still officially Bonn, with a population of about 300,000 and growing. The map of Germany shows that major cities pepper the banks of the Rhine from north to south. Hamburg, Frankfurt, and Cologne have populations of around one million, as does Munich in the south.

Other cities with populations between half a million and a million are Bremen, Dusseldorf, Duisberg, Essen, Hanover, Nuremberg and Stuttgart. Each is a major centre in its own right.

The city of Frankfurt is the major connecting point for the air routes which cross from east to west Europe. Its airport is second only to Heathrow in traffic volume in Europe.

Eastern Germany boasts industrial cities such as Leipzig and Dresden. Their industries are at present run down, inefficient and cause a lot of pollution. Some, such as the motor industry, have already ceased to function in the face of the vastly more modern Western products now available. However, these towns will, no doubt, resume their position as major industrial centres in the years ahead.

Major Industries

Germany participates in most modern industries, and is noted for engineering excellence in motor manufacturing, electrical and electronic products, machine tools and chemicals.

Economic Prospects

Germany's reputation for rapid and sustained growth is the envy of the world. However, there are some signs that this image is becoming slightly tarnished of late. The strength of the deutschmark, in particular against the US dollar, has badly affected the export of luxury durables, such as cars. Although German unemployment has been lower than the rest of Europe's, it was catching up before reunion, and complacency cannot be justified.

However, the Germans have weathered such storms before, and the immense strength of their economy still continues. Moreover, whilst union may have cost an awful lot, and may temporarily depress the economy, the new confidence and dynamism will undoubtedly bring Germany back even more strongly than before.

Other countries may catch up with Germany's progress, but it is unlikely that Germany will actually decline.

Educational System

Germany has a fine educational system. If you want your children educated in English, there are some English and American schools.

Again, as with France, it is quite feasible to have children board in the UK. The average flight time to northern Germany is one to one and a half hours and to south Germany about two hours.

Travel

There are no speed limits on the autobahns! This has become a very important right for many Germans, and suggestions to impose a limits are met with much wailing and teeth gnashing. There are advisory speed limits of 80 miles per hour, but these are not universally adhered to.

Germany has an excellent network of motorways, although these can become very crowded close to the cities at peak hours. German drivers are, on the whole, competent and courteous - but move over if you see lights bearing down on you on the autobahn, as he or she could be doing well over 120 miles per hour.

A car is quite important in Germany, which has so many small cities which are well spread out. There are beautiful places to visit very close to most cities, which are missed if you do not have wheels.

ITALY

Introduction

Italy has the second largest population of any country in Europe (57 million people), and a rich heritage. What is less often realised is that it is a serious and highly competent country, with a massive industrial base in the north.

However, the south of the country is still very under-developed, and this, perhaps, is where the country's lacklustre image originates. The economy is basically agricultural to the south and industrial to the north. Italy also suffers from chronic inflation problems.

The country has very few natural resources, and relies on trade to sustain itself. It is also heavily dependent on tourism - in many ways it could be described as the biggest museum on earth.

Italy has a deserved reputation for political instability, which continues today. However, this has little apparent effect on its industrial output.

Italy in its current unified form was established in 1861, when the ruling princes of the north and centre were deposed, and replaced by Victor Emmanuel II. Opera lovers will be familiar with the composer Verdi. The cry 'Viva Verdi' at that time was two edged, meaning also 'Viva Vittorio Emmanuale, Re d'Italia'.

The capital of the unified Italy at that time was the beautiful city of Florence - Venice and Rome became part of the country during the next ten years.

Italy, in common with its northern neighbours, tried to establish an empire, but with very little success. However, its imperialist ambitions were a contributory factor to the Second World War. In 1914, Italy started out as a neutral country, but joined the allies in 1915, and gained some territory as a result of the armistice.

Between the wars, Mussolini came to power, and led Italy into a pretty abortive campaign to conquer Abyssinia. This put the country at odds with most of the world except Germany, whose new chancellor, Hitler, formed an alliance with Italy. At the start of the war, Italy was forced to support Germany, and Germany tried to help further Italian ambitions in Africa. In the end this was to result in defeat. In 1943, Mussolini was deposed, and the allies invaded the south of the country.

The Germans, in a *Boys' Own* raid, freed Mussolini from an allied prison, and re-established him as a puppet leader in the north. They also put in an army to hold back the surging allied troops. As a result, Italy suffered horribly for the rest of the war, becoming one huge battleground.

After the war, a republic was proclaimed in 1946, which remains the system of government today. There are two chambers of government, elected by proportional representation, with an elected president.

The constant changes in government between the main parties, Christian Democrats, Republicans and Socialists have little apparent effect on the country, and constantly shifting coalitions are the normal order.

Opportunities in the Computer Industry

IBM has a good presence in Italy, as does DEC. Systems programming skills are always in demand, and there are also opportunities for those with a knowledge of the language.

Italy's Olivetti is a major force in the microcomputer market, and their products are in widespread use. However, they are (near as damn it) IBM compatible, using MS-DOS, OS/2 or Unix. Italian IT salaries are roughly comparable to UK IT salaries.

Language(s) Spoken

The main language is Italian, which has as many, and as complex, dialects as any European language. However, there are pockets of German and Serbo-Croat speakers in the border lands.

Italians are less versed in English than are northern Europeans, although it is the language normally taught in schools. To live there you must have acquired a working knowledge of the language. However, this is not as difficult as learning German or French.

It is not always certain that English will be an Italian's second language. I have had to have a technical conversation in French with an Italian, because that was our common language. Computer manuals and products, however, normally use English.

Currency

The Italian Lira stands at LL2145 to the pound.

Cost of Living

Italy's cost of living varies wildly. In the cities - particularly those frequented by tourists such as Rome, Venice and Florence - it can be very high. In less populated areas it is very low indeed. On average, though, Italy has one of the lowest costs of living in Europe.

Managerial salaries are, in common with most of Europe, higher than in the UK; other salaries tend to be the same or lower.

Local Taxation

Income tax rates start at 22 per cent and rise to 65 per cent, based on income. However, there is enormous scope for avoidance, and local accountants should be consulted.

The VAT standard rate is 18 per cent.

Housing

Housing can be quite expensive in the cities (where the work is likely to be found). A three-bedroomed apartment in Rome will cost around L1,300,000 per month.

Durables and food are, however, cheaper than in the UK.

Other Job Opportunities

In common with most European countries, there are some jobs with UK or American companies. However, there are not many opportunities for non-Italian speakers in Italy, and there is a very inefficient bureaucracy which must be bypassed to find them.

Work Permits

Although, in theory, no work permit is required, the Italian Embassy, in its reply to the survey for this book replied that one was necessary for British citizens. This was a surprise, and is wrong - however, it does perhaps illustrate the difficulty that expatriates might have in working in the country.

Educational Requirements

The same applies as with other EC countries. However, as indicated above, the Italians may not be quite as open to expatriates as the French or Germans.

Major Urban Centres

The country's capital, Rome, has three million inhabitants. It is the equivalent of London - the business and commercial centre of the country. The industrial centres in the north are Milan (with a population of one and a half million people), and Turin (with a population of one and a quarter million). The biggest centre in the south is Naples (which has a similar population size to Turin).

Other important cities are Bologna, Florence (Firenze), Genoa, Pisa, Taranto, Trieste and Venice. The southern part of the country is much poorer than the industrialised north - there is a definite north-south divide.

Major Industries

Italy does have a very impressive engineering industry, based in the north. It is well known for its motor manufacturing and for its office products company, Olivetti, which is one of the major players on the world stage.

The Fiat company, known for motor manufacture, is a conglomerate which owns many other types of industrial concern, including shipbuilders. In addition, it exports fine quality 'designer' products such as clothing, tableware and furniture. Fiat also exports food and wines; it now exports more wine than France.

Economic Prospects

Italy is always on the brink of financial ruin. It has the reputation for having a huge 'black' economy which keeps living standards up, but suffers from a chronic balance of payments deficit. Its two tiers (the rich north and poor south) are far more marked than in the UK, and there is bad blood between the regions. However, it has endured and muddled along somehow for many years, in this state, so will probably carry on doing so. It is still a major force in Europe.

Educational System

Italy has an education system whose efficiency varies by region. In the best areas, around Florence or Rome, for instance, it can be very good, but elsewhere it varies. Happily there are many British and American schools in the main cities.

Since boarding children in the UK is feasible the journey time to Rome takes just over two hours.

Travel

Italian roads are pretty good, although a toll is payable to use the autostrada (motorways). Petrol is more expensive than in the UK.

Although many makes of car are available in Italy, it is considered unwise to have too ostentatious a model, because of the danger of being kidnapped and held to ransom. This may be an overplayed scare, but many Italians stick to it.

Many cities (particularly the historic ones like Florence and Rome) no longer allow cars in the centre. The moped rules in such places, and swarms of them shoot down tiny streets like angry bees.

Italian trains are cheap, comfortable, and unpunctual. They very seldom leave on time, or from the expected platform. But that is the charm of the country. If you don't like it, don't go there.

BELGIUM

Introduction

Belgium is one of the smaller EC countries, but has a large influence because of the number of multinational companies which have established European headquarters there. Despite the country's relatively small size, its capital, Brussels is also the capital of the EC (along with Strasbourg).

Belgium has been part of many countries for much of its history. In the middle ages it belonged to Charlemagne's empire, then became relatively independent under the control of the Counts of Flanders before again being annexed by France in the fourteenth century. It was then successively ruled by the Hapsburgs and the Spanish (against whom the northern part rebelled to become today's Holland).

In 1794 it became French again, until 1814, when Napoleon fell. Only in 1831, following the London Conference, was an independent state established in the form of a kingdom. This remained intact despite the might of its neighbours until the First World War, when it became one of the main and bloodiest battle zones. Following that war, the country established links with Holland, which led to the modern problems of language. The northern Flemish speakers are at odds with the southern 'Walloons' - French speakers.

The country was again invaded by the Nazis in 1940 - on their way to defeat France. It was not completely cleared until after the war in 1945. Belgium was a founding member of both NATO and the EC - the headquarters of the former are in Brussels. It is also a member of the Benelux Union, joining it with Holland and Luxemburg.

The country is a monarchy, with a two chamber parliament, and a complex three level local government system. Its economy is heavily dependent on imported goods, and the services which are provided by virtue of its pivotal position on the European mainland.

Opportunities in the Computer Industry

Because of its many multinational headquarters, it offers good opportunities for computer staff with skills on mainframe equipment, whether or not they speak the language.

The market for IT people is still fairly buoyant and skills in the areas such as networking, relational databases and project management systems are in demand. IT salaries are substantially higher than the UK equivalents.

Language(s) Spoken

The country has two languages, in the south (Wallonia), French is spoken, and in the north (Flanders), Flemish. This causes much division. In effect, the two regions are occupied by quite different peoples, and are even governed by separate regional executives. So resented are the French speakers that it is often more acceptable to speak English in Flanders than French.

As with most countries, a knowledge of the local language is a great help. However, there are many companies with headquarters in and around Brussels whose main business language is English, and these are the major employers of freelancers.

Currency

The currency is the Belgian Franc. In February 1991 there were 60.43BF to the pound.

Cost of Living

Belgium's cost of living is significantly higher than the UK's, some 60 per cent higher in fact. To put that into perspective, a UK rate of £800 per week would need to be £1,300 per week to provide the same standard of living in Belgium.

Differences in costs are not uniform. Cars, for instance, are far cheaper - which led to the recent upsets when English companies tried to import cars from Belgium, massively undercutting UK prices. Other durables are similar in price to those in the UK, but food is far dearer. Without the UK levels of duty, alcohol - particularly wine - is relatively cheap. Petrol costs slightly more than in the UK.

Local Taxation

Taxes are levied progressively on income. However, there are many allowances, and if you do not permanently reside in the country you can receive substantial concessions. The result is that taxes in Belgium are almost as low as anywhere else in Europe.

As a member of the EC, Belgium levies VAT on goods. They operate a differential rate of six per cent on basic goods, 19 per cent on standard goods, and 25 per cent on luxury items.

Housing

There are no shortages of housing, although in Brussels the costs are somewhat escalated by the numbers of foreigners already there. Houses or apartments can be found through letting agents, or the press. Most apartments will be let unfurnished, and a typical price for a large one is 33,000 BF per annum. As in England, a deposit will be required against breakage and damage to the property.

Other Job Opportunities

Although DP jobs are relatively plentiful, others are not so easy to find - particularly if you do not speak French or Flemish.

Belgium's unemployment levels are relatively high, and there is great demand for jobs from the well-educated populace.

Work Permits

EC residents are free to enter and leave Belgium. However, the population carry identity cards, and one should be obtained from the local town hall within a week of arrival. A temporary card, valid for three months, will be issued initially, which may be extended by another three months if necessary (assuming you have a job). A normal identity card can be obtained after the six months.

Educational Requirements

As in other EC countries.

Major Urban Centres

The country is very much dominated by Brussels, with a population of one million. The other centres are Antwerp, with half a million people, Ghent, Liege and Charleroi. The total population of the country is ten million.

Major Industries

Belgium is a manufacturing and trading nation. Its only natural resource is coal, which is in decline. The main industries are engineering, chemicals and petrochemicals, electronics and car assembly. Agriculture is in decline, but Belgium is still producing nearly 80 per cent of its own requirements.

The majority of industrial growth is concentrated in the French-speaking areas. Because of this, French speakers are more likely to find opportunities than Flemish speakers - who should probably look for jobs in Holland.

Economic Prospects

Belgium is in the same boat as most EC countries in Northern Europe. They have experienced inflation - although this is now very low. They have high unemployment, at nearly ten per cent. However, their multinational employers in Brussels continue to sail through, and the future seems reasonably secure.

The inflation rate is lower than in the UK, and the country has a better trade balance. However, its growth rate has not equalled that of the UK in recent years.

Educational System

Apart from local schools, there are a number of international schools, which cater in the main for the American curriculum. There is a British School of Brussels, which has more than a thousand pupils, of all ages, as well as a number of other British schools. Children can board at most of these schools, although boarding in England is very feasible, since the air flight to Heathrow takes only 50 minutes.

Travel

Although a British driving licence is acceptable for up to three months, a Belgian licence is advisable, and may be obtained from a local town hall. The majority of journeys in this small country are likely to be by car or rail (the train system is good, and has links to all other European countries).

A good network of roads and autoroutes exists, and much of the traffic from England through to Germany passes through Belgium.

HOLLAND

Introduction

When American multinational companies decide to enter Europe, they often decide to start with Holland (the Netherlands). The country sits on the hub, with excellent

land, sea and air communications with the rest of the area
- including Scandinavia. Its inhabitants are known to be
generally multilingual, and friendly.

The country is small - and would be even smaller had not large
areas been reclaimed from the seas - and heavily populated,
with 15 million people living in an area of only 16,000 square
miles. In contrast, Switzerland is comparably sized, but has a
population of less than half. It is an impressive achievement,
therefore, that Holland is among the most prosperous
countries in the EC, per head of population, and that it hosts
some of the largest multinationals, such as Philips, Unilever
and Shell.

The last two names are joint British and Dutch companies,
and ties between the two nations are strong at all levels
- Britain is the major foreign investor in Holland, followed by
the United States.

Holland has a centrist government, and a benevolent but
expensive state, whose social services are generous and
humanitarian. Its libertarianism even extends to legalising
certain sorts of drugs, which puts it at odds with much of the
rest of the western world.

Holland also has the problem of a population growing steadily
older, as the birthrate declines, and general health improves.
For this reason there are fears that Holland may have to make
radical changes to its society in the near future. This is a
microcosm of the problems facing many of the older
democracies in Europe, including Great Britain, but is
exacerbated by the small size of the country.

The Low Countries has always been a prosperous part of
Europe, but it has had a great deal of blood spilt over it - being
controlled by the French and the Spanish in its history, and

sharing a king with England - William of Orange. Being a small sea-going nation, the Netherlands had, in its time, quite an empire. History has never entirely explained why the Dutch were so successful in annexing countries in the Caribbean and Far East. Perhaps it was because the country was so small, and, let's face it, uninteresting (a Dutch hill might just reach 100 feet), that its inhabitants needed to get away. Some became explorers, some artists (Rembrandt, Breugel).

Napoleon took the country over in the early nineteenth century, but France lost it on his downfall in 1814. The monarchy accepted very reduced powers, perhaps setting the trend for other constitutional monarchies like our own, in 1848. The system of government is a two chamber parliament. The monarch is very much one of the people.

The Dutch managed to keep clear of the First World War, but their country was invaded by the Nazis in 1940. They suffered badly in those days, and, although a friendly people, their opinion of Germans was tainted for many years.

The Dutch economy was founded on sea-going trade. The Rotterdam oil market spot price dominates world prices. It is a heavily industrialised country, with few natural resources except for natural gas.

Opportunities in the Computer Industry

Holland, like Britain, is the centre of an old empire on a huge and world wide scale. The Dutch are great seafarers, and Rotterdam is the largest port in the World. Modern ties with the EC, Benelux, the UN and NATO are strong. As a result there are many openings for computer staff, despite Holland's recent economic troubles - which have been worse than

Britain's. Holland is one of the most popular destinations for expatriate UK computer staff.

Holland offers some of the best rates of pay in the EC. An IBM analyst programmer could earn around £1,000 a week. This would go up to around £1,500 for someone with more specialised skills and could be anything from £1,500 to £2,000 for a consultant.

Language(s) Spoken

The main language, Dutch, is said by inhabitants to be the root for modern German, with which it has some similarities. However the second language for most Dutch people is English, and the Dutch have a deserved reputation as linguists. You will seldom find an educated Dutch person who does not understand English.

Knowledge of Dutch is seldom a prerequisite for contracts. However it is a courtesy to learn the language if you decide to go there, and local positions will require it.

Currency

The Dutch guilder stands at 3.35DFL to the pound. It used to be on a par with the German mark as recently as ten years ago, and a measure of the recent economic problems is the amount by which it has slipped since then.

Cost of Living

Dutch salaries, in common with most of Northern Europe, are generally half as much again as British, at all levels. However the cost of living is higher - not at German levels, but high enough. Food and durables are at higher levels than in the UK, but, once again, cars are cheaper.

Because of the heavily urbanised nature of the country, there are fewer regional differences in living cost. However the major urban centres (particularly Amsterdam) are the most expensive to live in.

Local Taxation

Income taxes are incremental, and although there are many allowances (including generous allowances to foreign nationals working for non-Dutch companies), they rise through a number of bands to almost the highest levels in Europe (to 72 per cent).

The social security costs are also very high - but benefits are also very much more generous than in Britain.

VAT is levied on all goods, at six per cent on essentials, 20 per cent on other goods.

Housing

This is the problem in Holland. There is simply not enough land to go round. There are continuous house building schemes in operation, and housing costs are not unacceptable - assuming that you can find an apartment in the first place.

A typical three-bedroomed apartment is likely to cost around 2000DLF per month, although, like Britain, there are houses for sale, at similar prices. The mortgage rate is lower in Holland.

Other Job Opportunities

There is a shortage of jobs generally, and the population is highly educated. There are opportunities, in the tourist industries and the multinationals, for native English, but a knowledge of Dutch would help.

Work Permits

The official line is that residence permits are seldom granted. however, like other EC countries, temporary residence after three months is simply acquired from the police, and permanent residence will be granted after five years.

Educational Requirements

As other EC countries.

Major Urban Centres

Amsterdam is the capital city, although the diplomatic centre is some distance away at the Hague - a delightful seaside town. Rotterdam is the largest industrial centre, and Utrecht houses many multinationals.

Major Industries

Although Holland has few natural resources with really only some natural gas, and salt, there are many industrial companies operating, in such areas as electrical and mechanical engineering, shipping, textiles, chemicals and diamonds (Amsterdam is the world diamond centre). Oil refinery and storage are so important that the Rotterdam spot price is quoted all over the world. In addition, despite its small area, Holland has an efficient and productive farming community - separate from its famous horticulture - with dairy products to the fore.

Economic Prospects

Holland has the same problems as Italy - a reliance on outside trade for its survival, because of few natural resources. However, that is as far as the comparison goes. The inflation rate is very low (below one per cent), and - although there are balance of payments problems, and an ageing population - the future looks reasonably assured. The Dutch are an industrious and highly educated people whose determination is shown by their refusal to let their country be overrun by the dark waters of the North Sea.

Educational System

Holland's educational system is competent and free. It is on a par with any in Europe. In addition there are international schools (British and American) in all the major cities.

Amsterdam is only 55 minutes away by air from Heathrow, so boarding in England is entirely feasible.

Travel

Holland is a small country, well served by road, train and air, and offering easy access to many other countries. The Dutch are, on the whole, courteous and restrained drivers. In the cities (and even between them, so short are the distances involved), the bicycle is the most favoured form of transport. Most main roads have cycle lanes alongside.

GREECE

Introduction

Greece is not really a viable place from the contractor's viewpoint. Although many would like to have an excuse to visit the country, the opportunities offered are very few and far between. Nevertheless, there are some possibilities with multinationals, or with British firms working in Greece. However, these operations will seem extremely parochial compared to those in the more developed countries.

Greece consists of the mainland, and large numbers of islands, from the tiny to the large (Crete is the largest). As a result, the Greeks have a highly developed maritime industry, with a large merchant fleet, and many passenger ships. The population of around ten million is mainly centered in and around Athens (one third of the whole), as is most of the business. The port of Athens, Piraeus, is one of the busiest in the Mediterranean.

Greece has gone through frequent political upheavals, only returning to democracy in 1974, when the military junta handed over power. Wherever you go, on the mainland or the islands, you cannot escape the politics, with the name of the ruling party (PASOK) painted on buildings, roads and even ancient ruins. Greece is now a full member of the EC.

Greece is becoming ever more popular with tourists, having matched, or even superseded Spain as the most visited holiday spot. This is a source of great regret for those who have loved the country for years, and seen it invaded by concrete hotels and discotheques. However, it is not difficult to understand its appeal.

Opportunities in the Computer Industry

Greece has a small computer marketplace. There are a number of UK and American companies with offices in Greece who have a small demand for staff, but there are few opportunities for expatriates.

It is hard to generalise on machine types, except to say that IBM is relatively strong, as is DEC.

Language(s) Spoken

The Greek language, which uses its own alphabet, is rather different from the ancient Greek taught at some schools. If you learnt that, you may be able to read the signs, but will probably not be able to communicate. It is worth picking up the Greek alphabet to be able to read the signs. Although many people speak English, German is more widespread these days, thanks to the holiday trade. Outside the towns, few people will understand you.

Currency

The Greek drachma stands at Dr297 to the pound.

As an aside, be aware that English banks will not normally exchange 1000 drachma notes.

Cost of Living

Greece can be very cheap indeed for everyday items. Food and drink, lodging and clothes are far cheaper than in Britain. All salaries are, however, proportionately lower. The cost of living is the lowest in Europe.

Durables are not so much expensive as almost unobtainable. Cars and petrol are very expensive - far higher than in Britain - as is car hire. Travel to the islands by ferry is cheap, even first class.

Local Taxation

Income tax, up to a top rate of 63 per cent, is progressively levied, but allowances are generous. Greeks are great avoiders of bureaucracy, so a cash economy thrives, particularly further from the centre.

Housing

Housing can be hard to find in the cities, although it is relatively easy in the islands. A guide price for a three-bedroomed apartment is Dr100,000 per month. Houses are very rare, and foreigners are very strongly discouraged from buying land.

Other Job Opportunities

In the main the best opportunities lie in the tourist industry. Throughout the summer, with an influx of about six million tourists, there is tremendous demand for guides. However, Greeks are given priority.

Work Permits

Since the beginning of 1988, the full EC provisions on the movement of labour have applied. However, you need a work permit, preferably before you leave the UK, and a residence permit before you can settle there.

Educational Requirements

In theory, the same as other EC countries.

Major Urban Centres

The main city is Athens, where almost everything is based, although Thessaloniki is growing in importance. Heraklion on Crete is also an important town.

Major Industries

Greece survives mainly through tourism, agriculture and shipping. Other industries are trying to gain a foothold, but are in the very early stages of development when compared to the rest of Europe.

Economic Prospects

Greece is an underdeveloped country. It has large mineral reserves, which have really not been tapped yet. Its political system is shaky, and it could revert to a dictatorship again.

Even Greece's membership of the EC is rather questionable - its commitment is not as strong as the northern European countries.

It is unlikely to see much growth, and its high rate of inflation shows no sign of reducing. Like the British economy it relies heavily on invisibles to counteract a truly awful negative balance of trade. However, it has little of the industrial development which could enable it to grow in the future.

Educational System

Most expatriates, unless they intend to go fully native, send their children to school at an English or American school in the capital. Boarding at home is possible - the flight time to Athens is two and a half hours.

Travel

There are fair roads, and good railway connections, as well as air and sea travel to the islands. The Greek idea of a motorway still tends to be a wide single carriageway, but with the truly breathtaking scenery, who's complaining?

SPAIN

Introduction

Spain is, in some ways, thought of like Greece - a poor relation, recently allowed into the EC, but with a very questionable political background, and little or no industry apart from tourism.

This view is partly accurate, but incomplete. Firstly, unlike Greece, Spain is a huge country, second in size only to France, with a population of nearly 40 million. It is a democracy, and has made great strides since Franco's death - although there are still strong right-wing pressures present.

Tourism is important to Spain, but so too is industry. Global car producers, Ford and General Motors have been manufacturing a good slice of their European output in Spain for some time, because labour is relatively cheap.

Spain has been one of the great world powers. It should be remembered that it was a Spaniard, Columbus, who discovered America, and another, Amerigo, after whom it was named. The Spanish lust for conquest and gold, allied to a frightening religious fervour, destroyed many of the ancient civilisations of South America, replacing them with often harsh and dictatorial governments which rule to this day.

Spain itself has a most unstable history. After the collapse of the Roman Empire, of which it was a part, Spain came under control of the Arabs. The effect of Muslim culture on much of the country can still be felt today. The Christian culture gradually took over and drove out the Muslims by the end of the fifteenth century. The last bastion of Islam, Granada, fell in 1492 - the same year in which Columbus discovered America. He was on his way to the east, to plunder for gold, and found an altogether richer prize.

The Spanish Hapsburg Empire covered almost as wide an area as the British were to control in the nineteenth century, but, like our empire, it began to fall apart under its own weight. There were reversals to its decline, but the final blows were dealt by Napoleon, with whom the Spaniards were forced to fight.

In 1923, a brief period of left-wing rule started, which was to lead to the Spanish Civil War in 1936. This was one of the turning points of modern history. German Nazis gained their spurs alongside Franco's fascists, fighting the less well organised communist brigades, made up of intellectuals and left-wing thinkers from many countries. The great American author, Ernest Hemingway described the tragedy of that war in *For Whom The Bell Tolls*.

Franco won the day, and remained in power until his death in 1975. Like many dictators, he gave little thought to who should be his successor, and King Juan Carlos was able to take over and establish a democratic monarchy. From this was formed the two chamber system of government (the 'Cortes' or Parliament) which rules today.

Spain has very quickly become one of the leading European democracies. In 1986, the country asserted by referendum its desire to remain in NATO (joined in 1982), but also expressed a desire to remove American bases from its soil.

Spain joined the EC in 1986. After a halting start, as its economy grasped the nettle, it soon established itself as one of the keenest members of that body. In the recent debates on British ERM membership, Spain was one of the strongest advocates of our joining.

Opportunities in the Computer Industry

Spain has a growing computer market, as its economy struggles to build up. However, it is fragile compared to the other major European countries, and, like Greece, offers few prospects for computer staff, except with multinational companies.

Language(s) Spoken

Spanish, by the end of this century, will be spoken by more people in the world than English, according to some experts. This is largely because of the huge population growths in middle and south America.

English is certainly understood by the well educated, but you really do need Spanish to live and work there.

Currency

The Spanish peseta stands at 184 pesetas to the pound.

Cost of Living

Like Greece, Spain's cost of living is low. Spanish cars and consumer durables are reasonably priced and available. Salaries are lower than elsewhere, except within multi-national companies.

Local Taxation

Spanish income tax is low, between 25 and 45 per cent. There are, however, a number of other taxes, such as wealth tax, and luxury taxes on houses but there are ways to avoid these, if you can prove that you spend less than six months in the country, for instance.

One reason that so many houses in Spain, perfectly built and luxurious, have half-finished sheds attached to them is to avoid this latter tax. If the house is unfinished the tax cannot be levied, therefore it is never finished.

The VAT rate is 12 per cent.

Housing

Buying property in Spain can be difficult. There have been many cases reported of people paying out, only to find that they own nothing at all. A local agent is recommended to deal with these. A guide price for monthly rent for a three-bedroomed apartment is 80,000 pesetas.

Other Job Opportunities

As in Greece, there are few opportunities outside tourism. However there are more multinationals which employ native English staff in some positions.

Work Permits

These are needed by everyone except artists. EC rules apply.

Educational Requirements

As in other EC countries.

Major Urban Centres

The capital city is Madrid. Other important cities are Barcelona, Bilbao, Malaga and Seville.

Major Industries

Tourism is one of the most important industries as is the motor manufacturing industry. Apart from Ford and General Motors, Spain has its own Seat, which was part of Fiat. Seat manufacture cars for home consumption and export.

Economic Prospects

Spain's prospects are not rosy. It has a large population to support, and chronically high levels of unemployment. There are some natural resources - Spain is a major producer of mercury, for instance. However, the economy is still basically under-developed, with a population which produces very little beyond its own needs. The government is making great attempts to foster its industry, and its efforts are paying off. Nevertheless, the country is still not broadly based enough. Moreover, the recent spate of dry summers has had the effect of reducing crop yields.

Nevertheless, some industrial sectors are growing, and Spain is said to have the fastest growing consumer electronics market in Europe.

Tourism has suffered recently. The Costa del Sol was the mecca for British package holidaymakers until recently. However, the flood has dried to a trickle in the last year or two. Analysts have tried to find a reason, but few have suggested the obvious.

Firstly, the country was becoming expensive, as its tourist-supporting infrastructure matured. However, the quality was not improving to match the price. The tourists have now moved on to Greece, which is much the way Spain was twenty years ago. Those of us who love that country can only hope that it is not as badly damaged as Spain.

The second reason is that air travel to Spain has become alarmingly unreliable, because of overcrowding and sheer bloody-mindedness by, amongst others, air traffic controllers. It is not unusual to be delayed for ten or more hours on any leg of a journey, and package customers suffer worse delays than anybody.

The third factor is the improved British climate, which has left many travellers wondering why they bother to go to the sun when they can find it at home.

Educational System

There are international schools in Madrid and Barcelona, and on the coast, to cater for the large numbers of expatriate British in the country.

Travel

Travel in Spain is a bit hit or miss. There are good through roads to the cities and the coast, but much of the country is very under-developed.

To foster the country's car industry there are restrictions on the import of cars. After six months a duty of 70 per cent is payable for residents' imported cars.

PORTUGAL

Introduction

Portugal is Britain's oldest ally - going back some 600 years. It is a small country, which you might expect to be overshadowed by its huge neighbour, Spain.

Portugal has a rich and separate existence, and has had an important role on the world stage in its time, colonising, for instance, Brazil, which still speaks the same language. However, it does share one thing with Spain: tourism.

Portugal is divided into a number of provinces, which include the Azores, and Madeira in the Atlantic ocean.

Opportunities in the Computer Industry

Except with subsidiary companies, almost none.

Language(s) Spoken

The main language is Portuguese. The second languages are Spanish and English.

Currency

The Portuguese escudo stands at 260 escudos to the pound.

Cost of Living

The cost of living is low, as is the general standard of living. The country is basically an agricultural economy, with very little indigenous industry. The country has the lowest per capita income in Western Europe.

Local Taxation

Income tax is low, but there are various complementary taxes in force.

Housing

Housing is cheap, particularly outside the main city of Lisbon. A guide price for a three-bedroomed apartment in that city would be around 55,000 escudos per month.

Other Job Opportunities

There are few opportunities outside the tourist industry.

Work Permits

Visas are needed for stays of longer than two months. Work or residence permits will need a letter of sponsorship from a company or individual resident in Portugal.

Educational Requirements

There are no specific requirements - and very few jobs for foreigners.

Major Urban Centres

Lisbon is the capital of Portugal and the most important industrial and cultural town, with a population of 820,000 people. Nearby Setubal is a rapidly-growing industrial town and an important centre for motor vehicle assembly.

Oporto is the major city in Northern Portugal - and is the centre textile and port wine production.

Major Industries

The main industries in Portugal are agriculture and tourism.

Economic Prospects

The Portuguese economy has improved since the days when inflation was galloping along at 30 per cent - it is now down to under ten per cent and through stringent methods the balance of payments deficit has been brought down. This improvement is partly due to its membership of the EC in 1986. Relatively backward agriculture has been brought up-to-date and much needed infrastructure has been built up.

Tourism, especially in the Algarve, has increased in popularity. On the negative side, Portugal is in danger of being flooded with a deluge of Spanish products, while it does not have much too compete with in the Spanish market.

Travel

The Portuguese railway system is extensive though there is room for some modernisation. Lisbon has an underground railway network.

Traffic is light and roads are good but narrow with lots of bends and a range of different surfaces. An International Driving Licence is useful.

SWITZERLAND

Introduction

Switzerland is recognised as having some of the most efficient services in the world - Swiss trains run on time, to the second, as they do in Germany. It also has a secretive banking system which, reputedly, defies the law. However, this is also neither unique nor entirely true if a crime has actually been committed. The Swiss is one of the leading banking systems in the world, and the country prospers hugely because of that.

That other symbol of Swiss efficiency, the watch, has been suffering at the hands of cheaper foreign products. The Swiss watch industry has hit back aggressively with the 'Swatch' products, which have been an enormous success.

Swiss neutrality is long established. The fact that this tiny, landlocked country, in the middle of Europe managed to remain neutral in the face even of Hitler is remarkable. The Swiss do not imagine themselves to be immune to the outside world, however, and all Swiss housing has to include a nuclear fall-out shelter. This is normally used as a spare room. It is no coincidence that the great symbol of neutrality, the red cross, is based in Switzerland.

Switzerland is broken into 16 'cantons', or regional areas, each with an elected assembly. The law can vary between canton, and there are, apparently, differences in banking law between the major cities as a result. One point to mention is that Swiss law, particularly with regard to banking, enshrines the principle of 'guilty until proven innocent'.

Switzerland has a unique history, in that it has been organised since the fourteenth century into its cantons, which have been able, partly because of geography, to fight off all opposition. Their army, made up of men from more than one canton, was one of the most powerful in Europe in the fifteenth and sixteenth centuries. When the Reformation swept through Europe, Switzerland was affected, and the country was badly mauled in the Thirty Year War - although it was officially neutral. Protestantism did not become completely established until the eighteenth century.

Switzerland became an intellectual centre in Europe, until it was annexed by Napoleonic France. In 1815, the independence of France was established, accompanied by an act of perpetual neutrality. However, the cantons bickered among themselves until the establishment of a federal system of government in the late nineteenth century.

The Swiss are not among the world's joiners. They do not belong to the IMF, UN, EC or the World Bank.

Opportunities in the Computer Industry

There are some DP jobs in Switzerland, normally with UK-based subsidiaries. The predominant machinery is IBM. Banking expertise is probably the most exportable.

Salaries are high in Switzerland - the highest computer contracting salaries are obtained in Switzerland although this is combatted by an expensive cost of living.

Language(s) Spoken

Switzerland borders France, Germany, Austria and Italy. As a result, it is a polyglot society, in which French, German and Italian are spoken.

The main language is German, followed by French, Italian (mainly close to the southern Italian border) and (a very small per cent) Romansch.

Many of the population speak more than one of these languages, and English is the main business language.

Currency

The Swiss Franc stands at SFr2.44 to the pound.

Cost of Living

Prosperous, yes. Expensive too. Switzerland remains one of the most costly countries in Europe - particularly in the glitzier places like Lucerne. Salaries are also higher, if jobs can be found.

Local Taxation

The rates of tax are generally lower than in the UK. However, the cantons also levy income taxes, which may rise as high as 15 per cent of income. As usual, the advice to foreigners is to use a local accountant.

Housing

Switzerland is a small country (15,493 square miles), with a population of 6.6 million people. It has also got a very high standard of living. As a result, housing may be difficult to find, and expensive. A guide price for a three-bedroomed apartment is around SFr5500 per month.

Other Job Opportunities

There are jobs to be found with multinational companies, but these are not plentiful. In addition, you may find occasional seasonal opportunities in resort towns.

Work Permits

The number of work permits made available is limited. However, there are opportunities with Swiss branches of UK or American companies. Because of the importance of banking both to the Swiss and the British, those with appropriate skills can find jobs in the same industry. Data processing is, of course, critical in the banking industry.

A knowledge of one of the main languages will help greatly (preferably German or French, depending upon the city; German for Zurich, French for Geneva or Lucerne).

There are a number of different types of permit:

- Type A permit is seasonal - temporary only. It is intended mainly for construction workers and tourists whose stay will be short.

- Type B is a temporary residence permit. It is valid for one year and only a limited number are available.

- Type C is a permanent residence permit. It may be granted after five years of legal residence for UK and other nationals (ten years to others), or to spouses of Swiss citizens.

Short term residence permits for a maximum of twelve months may be granted. These would be, for example, for work on a specific short term project.

You can also obtain a border commuting visa if you have lived for over six months in a border region, to enable you to work in Switzerland, but you must live outside Switzerland.

Educational Requirements

There are no specific requirements - but jobs are not plentiful.

Major Urban Centres

The capital is Bern. However, this is a relatively small city. Zurich is bigger and Geneva, Lucerne and Basle are all equally important.

Major Industries

After banking, Switzerland has thriving chemical, precision instruments and electrical goods industries as well as textiles and clothing - and, of course, tourism.

Economic Prospects

The Swiss economy still runs like their watches and trains, efficiently and on target. Because of the nature of the economy, it is pretty well insulated against world recession - and indeed has survived far worse crises than the present one.

Educational System

There are a number of English-speaking schools in Switzerland, and the native schools are of very high quality. Switzerland also boasts some of the finest universities in Europe, and has a very high level of technological training.

Travel

Apart from uncontrollable problems with the weather in the mountains, travel is easy and efficient. Switzerland, being landlocked and mountainous, can be surprisingly cold in winter to an English person. However, trains nearly always get through, and the roads are kept clear unless it is absolutely impossible to do so.

AUSTRIA

Introduction

Austria and Germany have been very closely allied in their history. However, before the last century, Austria was linked with the Hapsburg Empire. In the sixteenth century it was part of the empire including Spain, the Low Countries, southern Italy and much of the discovered part of the Americas.

During the eighteenth and nineteenth centuries it became the centre of the Austrian, then the Austro-Hungarian empire. At this time there was a flowering of the arts, particularly music, based in Vienna, which continues to this day.

After the First World War, the empire disappeared, and Austria became a republic. It was incorporated into the German Third Reich by the Austrian corporal, Hitler, in 1938 amid stage-managed scenes of ecstasy from its people. At the end of the war, it was liberated, and finally returned to its status as a republic in 1955. Its government is along the lines of most other European governments - a two chamber democracy.

There has recently been some unfortunate publicity surrounding the reputation of Austria's president, Kurt Waldheim, who has been accused of being an SS officer in the war, and knowing more about the actions of that body than he protests. The media abroad have, in effect, branded him a war criminal. However, his people have stuck by him, and the affair seems to have blown over for now.

One major difference between Austria and Germany is that, whilst the latter is split roughly half and half Catholic and Protestant, Austria is almost entirely Catholic. This has a cultural impact, more than anything else.

The Austrians seem a friendly and outgoing people, and more 'mediterranean' in outlook than their German cousins. Austria has announced that it intends to join the EC during the 1990s.

Opportunities in the Computer Industry

There are some opportunities, and the country is very prosperous. However, the extent of available jobs to outsiders - particularly non-German speaking - is fairly limited.

Language(s) Spoken

German. As in Germany, English is pretty widely understood.

Currency

The Austrian Schilling currently stands at 20.14 to the pound.

Cost of Living

The standard of living is high, and the cost is only moderate. It is a cheaper country to live in than its neighbour, Switzerland.

Local Taxation

The rates of tax are generally lower than in the UK. However resident expatriates (generally those who have lived there for more than six months) will be liable to tax on all their income, wherever earned, allowance being made to avoid 'double taxation'. If your company pays the rent on your apartment, this will be taxed (at 75 per cent of the rent paid) as income.

Housing

Housing is available, but not plentiful. It is not as bad as Switzerland. In the main cities, Salzburg and Vienna, it can be quite expensive and hard to find.

Other Job Opportunities

There are jobs to be found with multinational companies, but these are not plentiful. In addition, you may find occasional seasonal opportunities in resort and tourist towns.

Work Permits

There are limited work permits available. The country is not in the EC. Permits are issued on an individual basis to skilled labour. As a general rule the number of foreign workers in a company should not exceed ten per cent of the workforce.

Permits will be issued after judging the skill required and the professional qualifications needed to do a job.

Educational Requirements

There are no specific requirements - but jobs are not plentiful.

Major Urban Centres

The capital is Vienna. Other major towns are Innsbruk (a skiing haven) and Salzburg - where the composer Mozart spent much of his life.

Major Industries

The country has a mixed agricultural, industrial economy, and has some mineral resources.

Economic Prospects

Austria is very prosperous, with low inflation and unemployment rates.

Educational System

There are number of English-speaking schools in Austria, and the native schools are of very high quality.

Travel

Austria, like Switzerland, has a fair share of mountains, which can impede progress in the winter. However, there is more low-lying countryside, which is not quite so affected by the weather. Its climate at lower levels is pretty temperate.

CHAPTER 3

WORKING IN SCANDINAVIA

The Scandinavian countries of Denmark, Norway, Sweden and Finland occupy a rather different position from the rest of Europe - to use an awful modernism, their people have a different mind-set. This section does not include Finland, where there are very few opportunities. However, that country is very different - having a lot more in common with the Eastern Bloc, for which it has traditionally been a gateway to the west.

Denmark is an EC country, bordering other EC countries, and it has similar population densities to other EC countries. Norway and Sweden are very different - large landmasses, of which much is deserted, with small populations. Moreover, they have been able to assimilate some very progressive legislation, particularly with regard to all forms of equality of opportunity, which have great attractions to other Europeans. They have particularly efficient and caring economies, which seem to be able to deliver compassion alongside efficiency.

DENMARK

Introduction

Denmark is a Scandinavian country, but is also a member of the EC. It is therefore the gateway - both geographically and politically - between Europe and Scandinavia.

Denmark sits above Holland, on a group of islands linked together by road and rail bridges. The population is small -only five million. However, the Danes are not dissimilar to the Dutch, hard-working and efficient, and their economy shows this.

Copenhagen has a reputation as a really progessive city, more liberated or permissive even than Amsterdam.

Denmark was the centre of an empire which, under the well-known King Canute, stretched from England to the Baltic. This empire deflated inwards, as the Swedes and Germans asserted themselves, and the Normans overcame England. In the end, Denmark was left with Iceland, Greenland and some offshore islands, such as the Faroes, although they still controlled Norway before losing that country through their support for Napoleon. Denmark was invaded by the Nazis, and, in common with its neighbours, suffered at their hands.

Denmark is a constitutional monarchy, governed by a single chamber parliament.

Opportunities in the Computer Industry

Denmark is a relatively small marketplace. However, because of its multi-national nature, there are some opportunities for expatriate staff.

Language(s) Spoken

As with the Dutch, the Danes generally speak good English. However a knowledge of Danish will help in finding employment in this small country.

Currency

The Danish kroner stands currently at 11.27 kroner to the pound.

Cost of Living

Both the cost and standard of living in Denmark are among the highest in Europe, particularly in Copenhagen. This applies to nearly all goods.

Wages are higher than in the UK, at all levels, and workers enjoy better benefits - although tax levels are also high.

As you go further north, you must allow for the cost of heating the home. Denmark's climate is cooler than the UK's, and fuel is not cheap.

Local Taxation

Taxes in Denmark are the highest in the EC, with both local and state income taxes payable. The top rate of income tax just beats Holland's 72 per cent at 73.6 per cent. The VAT rate is 22 per cent.

Housing

Like Holland, accommodation is not expensive, but is hard to find. A guide price for a three-bedroomed apartment is 15,000 kroner per month. However, in central Copenhagen you will be very lucky to find a place at all.

Other Job Opportunities

Denmark is an international place, but has the normal problems of unemployment. There are not many jobs for foreigners. Multilingual Danes abound, and are more attractive to multinational companies than purely English speakers.

Work Permits

You need a work permit before moving in. This may be obtained by application to the Danish Embassy. You will also need a residence permit for stays of greater than three months. However, it is an EC country, and has, in theory, open borders to British workers.

Educational Requirements

There are no specific educational requirements, unlike Norway and Sweden.

Major Urban Centres

The major centre is Copenhagen, in which one million people live.

Major Industries

The British are very familiar with Danish dairy produce and bacon, and agriculture is still very important. However, new industries have been developed recently, particularly natural gas exploration. There are few large scale companies most are fairly specialised, like Bang and Olufsen, the specialist, quality electronics manufacturer.

Economic Prospects

Now that Denmark is able to produce much of its own fuel, it is not so sensitive to outside fluctuations. It has one of the highest growth rates in Europe at present.

However, like Holland, it has a small and ageing population, and a very active and paternalist welfare state which absorbs a lot of its GNP.

Educational System

The educational system is good, and there is an English school in Copenhagen.

Travel

The country is small. There is one major airport in Copenhagen. Internally there are good railways and roads. In Scandinavian countries, the rules on drinking and driving are far tougher than in Britain (see Norway).

NORWAY

Introduction

Norway is the long thin country which sits on the North Sea side of the Scandinavian peninsula. It is famed for its rugged landscape and fjords. Much of it is barren and uninhabitable - half the country lies above the Arctic Circle. Since it lies on the west of Scandinavia, it enjoys a slightly warmer climate than its neighbour, Sweden.

Norway had planned to join the EC at the same time as the UK, but this idea was rejected by a plebiscite of its four million inhabitants.

Although a small country, by population, Norway has a great deal of economic muscle now that its North Sea oil reserves are being exploited. It also has substantial natural resources, and plenty of hydro-electric power.

Norway was tied together with Sweden until 1905 when they declared independence and elected their own king, Haakon. He reigned for more than fifty years and was succeeded by his son, Olave. It is a constitutional monarchy, with a single chamber parliament. From 1935 until 1965, the country was governed by the left wing, apart from the period from 1940 to 1945, when it was ruled by a Nazi puppet, Quisling - whose name became synonymous with 'traitor'.

In 1965, the centre-right party took over from the socialists.

Opportunities in the Computer Industry

Norway, like Denmark, is a relatively small marketplace. The best opportunities for expatriate staff are in the oil-related industries.

Language(s) Spoken

Norwegian, similar to Danish and Swedish.

Currency

The Norwegian krone stood at 11.46 krone to the pound in early 1991.

Cost of Living

Salaries are higher in Norway than in Britain, but costs are even higher.

Local Taxation

Like Danes and Swedes, Norwegians pay for a benevolent state, in both local and national taxes. However, the highest rate of state tax is only 40 per cent - although the local tax is typically over 20 per cent. VAT is not applicable, although there are purchase taxes.

Housing

Norway has suffered from the 'Aberdeen effect' - housing is hard to find because of the oil workers. However, a guide price for a three-bedroomed apartment is 3900 krone per month.

Other Job Opportunities

There is an immigration embargo in force, except for workers employed in the North Sea oil industry. Apart from that, only specialists (such as computer personnel) will normally be allowed in.

Work Permits

There has been a stop on immigration since January 1 1975. Only skilled personnel who cannot be found internally will be admitted. Application for a work permit is therefore seen as an application for exemption from this 'stop'. As a result there are few expatriates working in Norway. A work and a residence permit are needed before entering the country. The former will not be granted unless the applicant can show that he or she has a job offer, and somewhere to live. Since Norway is not in the EC, the rules on mobility of labour do not apply.

Educational Requirements

You will need to be able to show that you have some technical qualifications before you are likely to get a job, except with a subsidiary operation.

Major Urban Centres

Oslo is the capital city, and has the dubious reputation of being the most expensive city in Europe. Other major towns are Bergen, Stavanger and Trondheim.

Major Industries

The dominant industry is oil. However, Norway's mineral deposits make it a rich source of such commodities as aluminium, iron ore, copper, zinc, and titanium. Norway also produces a large amount of paper and wood.

Economic Prospects

Norway is in the fortunate position of having abundant resources, and complete energy independence. It has a small population and low useable land mass, but can afford to pay for whatever commodities it needs. It currently has full employment, and wisely regulates immigration. Its foreseeable future looks secure, as long as the oil price holds up.

Educational System

Norway has a good education system and there are international schools in Oslo. Boarding in the UK is more normal - the flight to Oslo takes around two hours.

Travel

Climate is a major problem for travellers. The roads are adequate near Oslo, but not elsewhere, and may be snowbound for many days in the year. It is more normal to travel from town to town by sea.

Be aware that the Scandinavian countries have very strict drink driving rules. In Norway you will be gaoled, and have your licence suspended, if you have even the tiniest amount of alcohol in your blood. The rule is absolute - don't drink and drive at all.

SWEDEN

Introduction

Sweden has nearly twice the landmass of the United Kingdom - it is the third largest European country after France and Spain. However, like Norway, its population is small, since much of its mass is uninhabited. With eight million inhabitants, it has the lowest average population density in Europe. However, much of its peoples are concentrated in the south, in Stockholm, Malmo and Gothenburg.

From Sweden came the Vikings, who are credited now not so much for rape and pillage as for great voyages of discovery. They are said to have discovered America 500 years before the Spanish, and traces of their settlements have been uncovered there.

The Swedes controlled Scandinavia for hundreds of years, as well as parts of Russia. In the seventeenth century they were involved in the Thirty Year War against the Hapsburgs. This gave them control over Prussia and Pomerania - and the temporary position of a major European power. Russia and Austria, and then Napoleonic France were ranged against Sweden's empire, which was whittled away, until the country itself came under French control. Napoleon's downfall left only Sweden and Norway linked. Sweden's remaining German colonies were handed to Denmark, and Finland became controlled by Russia. The Norwegians became independent of Sweden in 1905. Sweden is a constitutional monarchy with a single chamber parliament.

Sweden has long been known as a mecca for freedom and socialism. This has given it both a highly civilised air and a problem. Sweden's socialist coalition, which governed from 1932 until 1976, was blamed for driving away many of the country's most gifted products, such as the film maker Ingmar Bergman, because of the very high levels of taxation. A period between 1976 and 1982 brought alternative government, and some relaxation of the rules. The socialist government is still in power, and the country remains one of the most civilised in the world, as well as enjoying high standards of living.

Sweden, like Switzerland, has been a neutral country for many years, and has not had a war since 1814. Its defence forces are strong and well organised, but it has remained aloof from world power blocs, being neither a member of NATO nor allied to Russia, nor is it within the European Community.

Sweden's neutral position is not one of weakness, but of strength, as was shown during the Second World War, and since in dealing with Russian incursions into its waters. It is no coincidence that the greatest prize for peaceful contributions to mankind, the Nobel, is Swedish in origin and management - although there is some irony in the fact that its named founder, Alfred Nobel, was a dynamite manufacturer.

Sweden's economy is highly successful. The country is rich in natural resources, and has a small population to feed. It boasts some extremely well established industries, which have been more successful than any in maintaining quality, whilst resisting the influences from the Far East. This is probably a result of Swedish management methods, which are probably the best in Europe, and a high level of technical sophistication. Although jokes are made about certain Swedish cars, their strength and quality is unquestioned. The harsh climate which makes such machines necessary has probably contributed to the lack of success of less substantial products from abroad.

There are many US and UK companies active in Sweden, helped by a government which welcomes foreign investment. With such a small population there is a natural skills shortage, and this is filled by foreign workers, mainly from other Nordic countries. There are many expatriate British in Sweden, and equally many Swedes in Britain (the Managing Director of the Santa Cruz Operation in the UK is a Swede, Lars Turndall).

Opportunities in the Computer Industry

Sweden has a well-established workforce, with good computing skills. Opportunities do arise, either with multi-nationals or on projects managed by British consulting companies.

Language(s) Spoken

The main language is Swedish. However, like inhabitants of other Nordic countries Swedes are gregarious and welcome foreigners.

Most Swedes speak English embarrassingly well, and often German and other languages too.

Currency

The Swedish krone stands at 10.95 krone to the pound.

Cost of Living

Swedes enjoy one of the highest standards of living in Europe, although costs are also proportionately higher. Nor is the country immune from the inflation which has affected other countries. Swedish salaries need to be about 15 per cent higher than their equivalents in the UK, and taxation is very high (see below).

Local Taxation

The Swedish socialist miracle has been sustained through high taxation. It is not at all unusual to pay more than 50 per cent of your salary in a very complicated series of taxes, including both state and local taxes. Because of the complex nature of the taxation system, and the regional variations, a local accountant is essential when preparing tax returns.

Housing

Sweden boasts very high quality housing, which is in reasonable abundance. Because of the harsh climate, houses are constructed very solidly and their quality is a watchword elsewhere in Europe. Windows, for instance, are triple or even quadruple-glazed.

This sort of thing does not come cheap, and housing costs are high - although not at the level of the major cities in Germany or France.

A guide price to rent a Swedish three room apartment is around 4000 krone per month. Official housing exchanges can help with finding accommodation in many towns.

Other Job Opportunities

There are some opportunities for spouses in the main cities, either with foreign companies or local companies with links abroad. However, the Swedes have a similar policy to the Norwegians. Only qualified personnel are normally given work permits. As a result the types of job open to foreigners are specialised or in the management of branch operations. There are few general vacancies.

Work Permits

Sweden is not an EC member, and those wishing to work there should obtain both work and residency permits before arrival. Unless you can show proof both of employment and a place to live you will not be allowed in. If you are married to a Swede, these restrictions do not apply.

Educational Requirements

As with Norway, you will need to be able to show that you have some needed technical qualifications before you are likely to get a post, except with a subsidiary operation.

Major Urban Centres

Stockholm is the major centre, where the majority of the posts arise. Gothenburg probably comes next for technical jobs, because of its outstanding university.

Major Industries

Sweden has a number of industries, but is perhaps best known for its cars, through Volvo and Saab.

Economic Prospects

The economy had been remarkably stable for many years until the early 1980s, when it suffered a downturn in line with most of the world. Although it is now prospering, its inflation rate is higher than before - although nowhere near the UK's.

Sweden has made a number of large company purchases recently, to gain a foothold in the EC before 1992.

However, in late October 1990, the Swedish interest rate was suddenly raised three points to 17 per cent - showing the poor state of the economy. The country also announced its intention to shadow the European Exchange Rate Mechanism (ERM).

Educational System

Sweden has a number of foreign schools, mainly based on the American high school system. If foreign children are sent to Swedish schools, special classes in the language can be laid on.

Travel

The comments for Norway apply to Sweden also. The Swedes converted to driving on the right some years ago, and they are are very safety conscious.

There is a good network of roads and these are kept clear, as far as possible, despite the weather. Note, however, that this country does stretch into the Arctic Circle, and road conditions in winter can be particularly harsh.

CHAPTER 4

WORKING IN THE
MIDDLE EAST

The Middle East has since time immemorial been at the hub of the trade routes which link the east with the west. As a result, its inhabitants have seen invasion from one side or another, and have watched a bewildering kaleidoscope of cultures pass through.

The great religions of the western world - Judaism, Christianity and Islam - have all arisen from the Middle East.

Arab merchants were reputed to be extremely rich. The tales of Ali Babar point to an incredibly prosperous group of people. Be that as it may, the vast majority of the world's main fuel lies in this area, and the resulting wealth is mind-blowing.

However, the countries of the area are, in the main, relatively newly established, many through casual favours, rather than along traditional borders. For instance, Iraq, although part of the area of ancient Mesopotamia, was only established as a state by the British early in this century as a gift to an Arab prince who had served them loyally.

The main religion of the area, Islam was established 600 years after Christianity, so it can be argued that it should be viewed in the same light as the latter in the fourteenth century. Then there were constant factional wars between fundamentalists and with other religions. It was arguably the bloodiest period of Christianity - in terms of wars fought for the sake of religion.

Some people see Islam as being a cruel or evil religion, but its doctrines are not dissimilar from Christianity, with some differences of emphasis and tolerances. The fundamentalists are not representative of the majority, just as the Spanish Inquisitors did not represent all Christianity. Unfortunately, because of the conditions of the area, any warring bully who wants to establish some tenuous claim on another's land or property is likely to try to make out a religious case for his actions.

Sadly, there have been many sufferers from this sort of intolerance. The city of Beirut was once a jewel of modern comfortable living. Now it is a war-torn hulk, thanks to the combined efforts of Arabs and Jews. The lovely, prosperous, little country of Kuwait has fallen under the heavy hand of dictatorial tyranny, and has been torn apart in the same way. The sufferers are, as always, the ordinary decent people of the areas concerned.

Because of the rapid increase in the world's requirement for oil, and the resultant growth of oil rich economies almost from a standing start, the area has been an incredibly fertile one for experts of all types from Europe and America. Construction workers, engineers and computer staff have all been lured by huge salaries, often virtually tax-free, to do short contracts, take the money and run.

Before the Iraqi invasion of Kuwait, this was beginning to slow down. The major countries had encouraged the training of indigenous staff, and needed less foreign help. The result was that earnings were reducing, and, because conditions were not particularly friendly, there were less people willing to go over there. Naturally, this was a trend, and there were still plenty of jobs available - though the numbers were reducing.

The Iraqi invasion left many westerners stranded in Iraq or Kuwait, and a lot who did escape came back home with very little to show for their time out there. Public schools have been coping with the fact that a number of their pupils have been, or will be withdrawn because their parents can no longer afford the fees.

However, because staff have terminated contracts in neighbouring countries, and because new workers are not too keen to enter an area of uncertainty even after the ceasefire, there are opportunities to earn good money in countries like Saudi Arabia, if you are prepared to accept the risk. Whether this state of affairs will still pertain when this book has been printed is another question, however.

Up to, and during the war to liberate Kuwait, many embassies in London had signs warning their nationals not to enter any of the Middle Eastern countries listed here at the moment. Check with them on the present situation.

Europeans may find other Europeans slightly different in attitude. The north-south divide is particularly strong. However, the differences tend to be ones of emphasis rather than fundamental belief. Arabs, on the other hand, enjoy a quite different culture from ours, as the American troops in Saudi Arabia found. There are many points of etiquette to bear in mind when dealing with Arabs. However, these need not be overstated, since Arabs are as well travelled as westerners (indeed often more so), and quite accustomed to our ways.

Most British consulates will provide guidelines for dealing with the local people. There are a few obvious points, particularly with regard to women. Arabs are not so tolerant as we are towards women, regarding them as chattels and requiring them to cover themselves in public. This can be very unsettling, particularly to western women, and is, to most western eyes, pretty offensive. However, it is necessary to be aware of their views, even if you do not agree with them, as you will otherwise find it impossible to operate in the country.

You may find that you are not able to enter an Arab country if you have an Israeli or South African stamp on your passport.

This applies to the United Arab Emirates. Because of the relative instability in the area, you should check this rule, if it could apply to you, before making your application.

One other effect of the crisis has been to prevent the quotation of exchange rates, therefore those shown are approximations.

BAHRAIN

Introduction

Bahrain is a group of 35 islands in the Arabian Gulf, 16 miles from the east coast of Saudi Arabia. The main island has its own fresh water supply. It has a very small area of land (264 square miles), and a population of only 417,000 people. The capital is Manama. Immigrant workers of one kind or another constitute around 50 per cent of its workforce. The country is governed by a monarch and has no democratic institutions.

Bahrain is more relaxed than its neighbours in observation of muslim customs. Expatriates are able to enjoy a similar way of life to normal with less restrictions.

Opportunities in the Computer Industry

After the crash in the oil prices in the mid-1980s opportunities became much more limited than they had been previously. Many of the opportunities are for permanent staff rather than for contracting. IT jobs tend to require good technical skills and are involved with building up the infrastructure of the country and developing a variety of services such as department stores.

Salaries in IT are still good as they are tax-free but they are not usually higher than those available in Europe. Perks such as free accommodation, free airfares, free healthcare and good bonuses are attractive.

Language(s) Spoken

Arabic, with English as the international business language.

Currency

The Bahrain Dinar stood at BD0.61 to the pound at the beginning of 1991.

Cost of Living

The cost of living is low - most foreign jobs will include accommodation, medical insurance, a company car and help with schooling as well as paid trips home. However, essentials do cost more (almost double UK prices).

Local Taxation

There is no local taxation, and no limit to the amount of money which can be sent abroad.

Housing

See the Cost of Living section.

Other Job Opportunities

It is unlikely that your (female) spouse or partner will be able to find work except with a multinational company.

Work Permits

Expatriates represent the majority of the population. Therefore the government is quite used to dealing with visas. In general, these will be arranged by your employer, and will not present a problem to suitably qualified personnel. They are renewable yearly. For stays of up to thirty days no visa is needed, after which you will need a residence visa.

Educational Requirements

None specifically.

Major Urban Centres

The capital is Al Manama with a population of around 100,000 people; all the main activities centre around it.

Major Industries

The oil industry is naturally the base industry but Bahrain is also establishing itself as an industrial power using its petro-revenues.

New industries which are being developed include ship-building and aluminium smelting.

Economic Prospects

The main question mark arises from the position of Saudi Arabia - linked by causeway to the main island. If that country remains stable, Bahrain's prospects look good. The other area of uncertainty comes from the potential activities of Shi-ite fundamentalists, although these do not appear to present a real threat at the moment.

Educational System

There are a number of English-speaking schools available, and boarding schooling may well be paid for by the employer.

Travel

It is a small landmass served by a good modern road network. All Bahrain's islands are connected by motorboat or dhow.

EGYPT

Introduction

Egypt is one of the ancient countries of the world. Its history is inextricably linked with biblical figures such as Moses. It is as important now, in a Middle Eastern context, as it was then.

Egypt, after its period of independence in biblical times, when the pyramids were built for its fabulously wealthy rulers, became a land to be governed and fought over. It was a major slice of the Roman empire, and after that collapsed, remained part of the Byzantine Eastern Empire, before falling to Arab conquerors. It belonged variously to the Ottomans, the French and then the British - who took over to protect the newly completed Suez Canal in 1882.

Egypt became independent - in theory at least - in 1936, but the British presence was still very strong, particularly in the Second World War.

In 1956, a revolution led by the formidable Gamal Abdel Nasser brought about the Suez crisis, in which a French-Israeli force tried to depose Nasser. Nasser won the day, and his standing became very high. He was seen as a potential leader of a free Arab nation. However, the Arabs could not agree among themselves, nor could they accept the presence of Israel. In 1967, the Six Day War lost the Sinai peninsula and Gaza strip to the Israelis. A further war was fought between the neighbouring countries (Yom Kippur in 1973), and a peace treaty - the Camp David accord - signed in 1979 returned the ceded lands to Egypt. The president of Egypt at that time was Anwar Sadat. He was assassinated by fundamentalists in 1981, and the current president, Mubarak took over.

Egypt has been a vital force in keeping the peace with the West in the last decade, and continues to be a stabilising influence in the present troubles. It is a presidential democracy (there are not many in the Middle East), and receives a great deal of American aid (it is second only to Israel in this respect). Its major export is oil - although this is now falling in volume.

It is one of the most populous Middle Eastern countries - it is estimated to have a population of 52 million people and increasing rapidly. However, it has not yet begun to build a manufacturing economy.

Opportunities in the Computer Industry

Opportunities are limited due to the huge indigenous population. The posts available tend to very technical and permanent.

Language(s) Spoken

Arabic, with English as the international business language.

Currency

The Egyptian Pound currently stands at LE5.85 to the pound.

Cost of Living

Egypt's cost of living is not too high, as long as you stick to locally produced foods, which are much cheaper than their UK equivalents. Accommodation is not too expensive; a guide price for a three-bedroomed apartment is around LE2400 per month.

Local Taxation

Expatriates are liable to income tax at 22 per cent, but there is a double taxation agreement with Great Britain. If you are resident for less than six months, the tax rate is a flat ten per cent on your total compensation including expenses.

Salaries are much higher - you may get more than twice as much for an equivalent job as the salary in the UK. It is normally possible to be paid at least a part of the money outside Egypt - which can greatly reduce the tax burden.

Housing

Housing is available, and can normally be arranged by an agent or employer.

Other Job Opportunities

It is unlikely that your (female) spouse or partner will be able to find work except with a multinational company.

Work Permits

These are not needed for short term assignments (less than a month). After that you will need a sponsor to show that no local person can do the same work. Visas are relatively difficult to obtain. They will initially be granted for ten months, and are easily renewable thereafter. The proportion of foreign workers is limited to ten per cent of the company's total manpower, and 20 per cent of payroll costs. In addition, only 25 per cent of a company's administration and professional employees can be expatriates, and 30 per cent of wages paid to foreigners in those categories. Expatriates with work permits may be accompanied by their spouses.

Educational Requirements

None specifically.

Major Urban Centres

Cairo is the heart of Egypt. Estimates of its population range from 11 to 14 million people - about a quarter of Egypt's whole population.

Other major cities are Alexandria, the largest Egyptian port, and Aswan.

Major Industries

Agriculture is still the main industry although Egypt has a fledgling oil industry. Attempts to lay down a manufacturing base have been largely thwarted by the massive increases in the population.

Economic Prospects

Egypt's economy is not one of the healthiest. However, its relative political stability makes up for this. It is unlikely that the fundamentalists will take over the country.

Its growing population is a cause for worry - there are many mouths to feed. It needs to build up its industrial infrastructure pretty quickly.

Educational System

There are a number of English-speaking schools available. However these are not cheap, and it may be just as good to send children to an English boarding school.

Travel

Egypt has an extensive public and private transport system. Trains and buses travel to most cities and towns.

Egyptian driving is very hectic and impatient - the sound of the horn is very common in any stream of traffic. Surprisingly, accidents are not too common.

KUWAIT

Kuwait has just been freed by the Allied forces and the major job of rebuilding the shattered country will soon begin.

In six months or so, opportunities will probably be good, as will salaries, for many IT staff will be required to recreate a modern infrastructure for this cruelly devastated country.

SAUDI ARABIA

Introduction

Saudi Arabia is one of the largest Middle Eastern countries - nearly two and a half times bigger than Egypt - but has a small population of only 15.75 million inhabitants. It has the world's largest known reserves of crude oil, and is the largest producer apart from the Soviet Union. Its whole economy is based upon oil. The country is mainly desert, and was for centuries part of the Ottoman Empire. During the First World War, the British helped the Arabs to rise up against the Turks and create the modern state.

Saudis are strong muslims, of the Sunni persuasion, as befits the home of Mecca. Those contemplating working in the country must be prepared to put up with a very restrictive regime in which alcohol is banned, and women are very much chattel.

There is great antipathy to Israel and South Africa, but the country is closely allied to the West. Its government is monarchist, with no democratic institutions. It still has a reputation for inflicting harsh punishment on offenders (like cutting off the hand of a thief). Westerners have been severely punished for perceived sexual or alcohol-related crimes.

The sorts of salaries which could be earned in Saudi Arabia used to be quite fabulous - sometimes as much as three times UK equivalents, and tax-free. This has made the place very attractive to those who want to build a nest egg. However, the bubble was, if not bursting, certainly beginning to deflate, before the Iraq invasion of Kuwait and the subsequent Gulf War. That has put Saudi Arabia in some apparent danger (although the threat is well contained now that there is such a large US presence), and the signs are that employers and their agents are prepared to pay very high sums to attract workers. Salaries are reputed to have jumped up more than 20 per cent since the invasion.

Opportunities in the Computer Industry

Many of the positions on offer are for permanent staff rather than contractors. The main areas of work tend to be involved in building up the modern infrastructure of the country such as in communications and hospitals. These posts are usually technical, requiring senior programmers and analysts.

The system which often works is that if there is a vacancy in a local company a Saudi Arabian software house will act as the middleman and will find someone, such as an expatriate, to fill the post.

As noted for Bahrain, although salaries are no longer markedly higher than in Europe in normal circumstances, perks such as free accommodation and the fact that everything earned is tax-free can be a good incentive.

Language(s) Spoken

Arabic, with English as the international business language.

Currency

The Saudi Ryal stood at 7.1 to the pound.

Cost of Living

The range of fringe benefits offered to expatriate staff is similar to those in Bahrain - free accommodation and schooling, etc. This makes the cost of living relatively low.

Local Taxation

There is no local income tax, nor restrictions on taking money abroad.

Housing

Normally provided by employers.

Other Job Opportunities

Virtually none for females - who will find the attitude towards them offensive and repressive.

Work Permits

Work permits are required, but will be arranged by an agent or employer. The work permit is needed before a visa can be provided, and this can take quite a long time.

Educational Requirements

None specifically.

Major Urban Centres

Riyadh is the capital and largest Saudi city. The cosmopolitan city of Jeddah is the country's major port. Dhahran is an important oil town.

Major Industries

Oil is the backbone of the Saudi economy. It is using profits from this to develop a modern and sound infrastructure through the expansion of industries such as electricity and telecommunications. A number of agricultural schemes have also been successfully initiated through the use of revenue from oil.

Economic Prospects

Although it has suffered a relative recession in recent years as oil prices have eased a bit, Saudi Arabia is still very strong economically. If there are clouds on the horizon, these are caused by its monarchist government. There is always the danger of fundamentalism.

If the country were to be taken over, either from inside or by Iraq, the world would reel because of the shock effect on oil prices. That is why so many men and arms have flowed in during the Gulf Crisis - it is essential to the economy of the western world to keep Saudi Arabia stable.

Educational System

Similar to that in Bahrain.

Travel

Oil revenues have been used to finance good and cheap transport including the building of many new roads. There is also a railway system. Riyadh and Jeddah have both got modern airports.

UNITED ARAB EMIRATES

Introduction

There are seven Emirates, small sheikhdoms, of which Abu Dhabi (the largest city) and Dubai are the best known and most prosperous. Although they have been more or less fused into a single unit since 1971, there are still occasional disputes between them. Apart from the cities, most of the country is desert, and there is quite a problem with providing sufficient water.

The government consists of a Supreme Council of Rulers, who are unelected heads of the emirates. There is no democratic ruling body.

The cloud on the horizon, as always, is fundamentalism. The UAE, like Bahrain, is potentially quite vulnerable to hostile invasion from Iran or Iraq. However, this should not be overstated. Although Saddam Hussein has claimed Das Island, it is a long way away, and therefore seems an unlikely place for Iraqi aggression to reach.

The economy of the Emirates is still oil-based, although this has spawned a number of development projects, introduced by Western companies.

Opportunities in the Computer Industry

The opportunities for IT staff are very similar to those in Bahrain and Saudi Arabia. Similarly also, salaries no longer tend to be fabulously high but they are still tax-free and perks such as free accommodation are the norm.

Language(s) Spoken

Arabic, with English as the international business language.

Currency

The UAE Dirham stands at ADH7.17 to the pound.

Cost of Living

The same remarks apply to UAE as to Saudi Arabia and Bahrain, with regard to housing and fringe benefits.

The cost of living is very high, particularly in the main cities.

Local Taxation

There is no local income tax.

Housing

See Saudi Arabia and Bahrain.

Other Job Opportunities

There are a number of possibilities for secretarial and other jobs - the attitude towards women is much more relaxed than in Saudi Arabia.

Work Permits

UK passport holders have a right of entry, and can obtain both work and residence permits on application from their employer. The situation is relaxed, and there are plenty of opportunities.

If you wish to bring your family in, each member needs to be applied for, and specifically named (including dependent children).

Educational Requirements

None specifically - indeed all manner of employees can move into the country.

Major Urban Centres

Dubai is the major city and it is also one of the most important commercial centres of the Middle East.

Major Industries

Oil, like most of the Middle East, although its manufacturing base is growing through development projects.

Economic Prospects

Although there has been a relative downturn recently, the Emirates still earn enormous oil revenues. Their offshore installation at Das Island is producing well, and exploration continues.

Educational System

There are a number of English schools, and schooling may be paid for by an employer.

Travel

Roads are good and there is a limited bus services but there is no rail network.

CHAPTER 5

WORKING IN AFRICA

It may be an unpopular view, but Africa is still very backward. Opportunities do exist for computer staff, but, in general, these are restricted to a few prosperous countries - others are really only exceptions at present.

There are African countries which do offer opportunities, notably Nigeria, an oil-based economy, and South Africa, which, whatever the politics of the situation, is the major economic force on the continent, and a haven for many British. Included also is Kenya; although the opportunities are relatively few, it has been a more successful country in the past.

KENYA

Introduction

Kenya was one of the most successful British colonies, with some of the best farming land. Independence came in 1963, after much bloodshed, including the Mau Mau wars in the early 1950s.

The government of Jomo Kenyatta which took over then has continued in power (now under Daniel Arap Moi). The ruling party is the Kenyan African National Union (KANU), which has been riven by internal fights and attempted coups.

The economy is largely agricultural, producing tea and coffee - the main exports - and other crops. The constantly fluctuating nature of the commodities markets has an effect on this economy, making it quite unstable. Naturally it is affected by weather, and the recent droughts have hit the economy quite hard.

Opportunities in the Computer Industry

Opportunities are limited but available to most levels of good computing personnel. Multinational subsidiaries are the main employers of foreign staff. Communications skills are most in demand.

The salary levels are not much greater than in the UK but the perks with the job such as free accommodation and leisure facilities are excellent.

Language(s) Spoken

Swahili is the national language and English the official one.

Currency

The Kenyan shilling (Ksh) stood at 45Ksh to the pound at the beginning of 1991.

Cost of Living

Because of deep seated inflation, and food shortages, the cost of living is quite high.

Local Taxation

There are local taxes on an increasing scale.

Housing

There is no shortage of housing, even in the capital, Nairobi, and many employers will provide accommodation.

Other Job Opportunities

There are opportunities, particularly for reasonably qualified people in the city with multinationals.

Work Permits

UK and Commonwealth citizens do not need a visa, and in general entry is not a problem, as long as you can show that you will benefit the country's economy.

As unemployment is growing, work permits may be more difficult to obtain and bribes may be necessary.

Major Urban Centres

Nairobi, the capital, is a modern city.

Mombasa, 300 miles from Nairobi, is the second largest city and the chief port of Kenya.

Major Industries

The economy relies largely on its agriculture. There is some economic development in its manufacturing sector.

Educational Requirements

None specifically.

Economic Prospects

The country's chronic balance of payments deficit and fluctuating income make it somewhat unstable. It is hard to forecast how it will develop.

Educational System

There are independent schools in the country for expatriates.

Travel

The trunk roads between the main cities and towns are good quality but elsewhere deteriorate, especially in the rainy season. Kenya Airways runs an extensive internal air service.

NIGERIA

Introduction

Nigeria is one of the most populous and prosperous black African countries, with an oil-based economy. It has been independent of Britain since 1960, and has undergone a number of bloody civil wars since then, the most dangerous of which was the Biafran war in 1970.

The government is a dictatorship, led by President Ibrahim Babangida, who came to power in a coup in 1985.

The country is, in fact, quite stable, and there are many British expatriates living there.

Opportunities in the Computer Industry

Opportunities are fairly limited but available to all levels of good computing personnel. Contracts are most frequently with international companies who have a post to fill in one of their African subsidiaries or need someone to go out on a maintenance contract.

Companies who require people include the major oil companies, such as Shell, and communications companies. Telecommunications skills are presently very marketable as the more prosperous African countries build up their infrastructures.

Contracts are normally of at least a year's duration and IT salaries are comparable to those in the UK and for a permanent post such as communications engineer the salary will be around the £25,000 mark. An average figure for contractors is around £12 to £13 per hour.

The real difference is the excellent perks which go with the salary. These frequently include housing, often in a special foreign compound, a subsidised telephone bill, a car (perhaps) with a full-time driver, and sometimes a cook and cleaner. Other perks may include free use of leisure facilities within the compound.

Language(s) Spoken

The official language in English, although there are about 250 local languages spoken by the people of Nigeria.

Currency

The naira (N) stood at N8 to the pound in early 1991.

Cost of Living

The cost of living is high - Lagos is quoted as being second only to Tokyo, although, not surprisingly, petrol is cheap. You will need a proportionately higher salary to live there than in the UK.

Local Taxation

Local income taxes are lower than UK taxes.

Housing

Expensive and rare. Guide price for a three-bedroomed apartment is N8,000 per month - and you will have to pay for up to five years' rent in advance. However, employers usually provide housing.

Other Job Opportunities

There are many multinational companies, and work can be found.

Work Permits

Residence permits can be obtained by employers.

Educational Requirements

None specifically.

Major Urban Centres

Lagos is the capital and the largest town. It is also a well-equipped port. Kano is the principal commercial centre of northern Nigeria.

Other large cities worth mentioning are Port Harcourt, Ibadan and Abeokuta.

Major Industries

Oil and gas are both crucial industries in Nigeria. Agriculture is very important. The chief exports of Nigeria include cocoa, mineral oil and timber.

Economic Prospects

Nigeria is an oil-based economy now, and has huge reserves of natural gas still to exploit. Despite this, the government is trying to reduce their reliance on this resource, and to switch back to the previously agricultural bias. This is a sound policy, and prospects look pretty fair.

Educational System

There are independent schools in the country for expatriates, although many send their children to boarding schools in the UK.

Travel

Nigeria has quite an extensive network of railways and roads; this network does peter out in more remote areas where more roads need to be built. There is also a serviceable air network and a useful number of waterways.

SOUTH AFRICA

Introduction

Like it or hate it, South Africa is a haven of prosperity. Its white government sits on some of the richest land in the world, and has created a highly profitable country. The only mineral wealth which it does not possess is oil.

To understand South Africa, you must go back to its origins. The Cape area was settled in the seventeenth century by the Dutch, who set up a victualing station for the Dutch East India Company.

The British came in the early nineteenth century and established a British colony. The Dutch 'Voortrekkers' were less than happy. They moved north, inland and set up independent republics called the Orange Free State and the Transvaal. In the process they felt under pressure to subdue African tribesmen.

In 1869, diamonds were discovered in the Transvaal - later gold was also found. This set up a rush of prospectors and fortune hunters, many of whom were British. The Transvaal president, Paul Kruger, tried to control the situation, but merely inflamed the British into a fight. The Boer war was won by the British in 1902. It was a guerrilla war, with non-uniformed troops fighting a trained army, as they had in the American War of Independence. The British used all sorts of tactics, including concentration camps for prisoners.

The Union of South Africa was established in 1910, uniting the country. In 1948 the National Party came to power, and rules to this day. This party built up the mechanism of apartheid, or separate development, to control the far more numerous (in a ratio of 5:1) black population.

Black South Africans are actually more prosperous than many black people in neighbouring black states, but the system of apartheid is quite unacceptable to most of the world's community. As a result, there have been sanctions against South Africa for many years - which have had limited effect. The country has a parliamentary 'democracy', for which only the whites can vote, with a separate chamber for coloureds (mixed race) and Indians. Blacks (Bantu) are still excluded from power but that should not last.

There has been a lot of violence in South Africa in the last few years, and it is by no means over yet. So far it has been contained mainly in the black townships by a notoriously brutal police force. However, all that could easily change.

South Africa's enormous mineral wealth, as well as a cheap and subservient workforce, has kept it well up in the league of rich nations. It has suffered some decline recently, largely because of oil prices, but is still very prosperous.

Living in South Africa can be exceedingly comfortable. Because of the abundance of cheap labour, you can be waited on hand and foot if you want. The climate is generally excellent (it is warm, but not oppressive in the summer, and relatively mild in the winter). The scenery is fabulous - just drive out to the edge of the high Veldt and look over at the middle and low Veldt in front of you for the most gorgeous views. It is like living in a very comfortable modern European country (the roads, for instance, are excellent) with the luxury of the old colonies.

However, the downside is that, if you have scruples, South Africa is not for you. The differences between blacks and whites are very marked. Whilst the whites live in modern well-appointed houses, their 'servants' (often little more than slaves) are forced to live in hovels at the bottom of the garden. Beside camp sites you see signs saying 'No Dogs, No Servants' - dogs come first. If the blacks are better off than they would be in other states that is no defence for such treatment, they could be as well off without being oppressed.

Things are changing. The release of Nelson Mandela was a good sign of a thaw. The current president, de Klerk, is clearly trying hard to free things up and has recently stated that he will abolish apartheid laws. However, the spectre of the extreme right wing hangs over all.

Opportunities in the Computer Industry

South Africa has a thriving and modern business community. There are many computer opportunities. Although IBM sold its subsidiary there some years ago, there is plenty of IBM, DEC and ICL kit.

Be aware that some people in this country are so fervidly anti-apartheid that you may find quite a lot of prejudice against you if you return and tell people where you have been working. It could also cause problems if you want to go on and work in other countries in Africa or the Middle East.

Language(s) Spoken

English and Afrikaans. The latter is like Dutch. It is not spoken everywhere, and most South Africans speak English. However, Afrikaans is taught in schools.

Currency

In early 1991, the South African rand (R) stood at R4.95 to the pound.

Cost of Living

The cost of living is lower than in the UK. South Africa is largely self-sufficient (except in oil), and the quality of food is very good. There is a motor industry, and electrical goods are not wildly expensive.

Housing (see below) is also relatively cheap. If you do not mind the thought, servants can be hired extremely cheaply, too.

Local Taxation

Income tax is fairly heavy and progressive, and there are other taxes such as VAT and import duties on foreign goods.

The overall taxation position is more favourable than in the UK.

Housing

A three-bedroomed house (there is plenty of space, and little need for apartments) would rent for around R1200 per month. However, rented property is scarce, and most people buy their houses.

Other Job Opportunities

There are plenty, particularly in the cities.

Work Permits

The South African government encourages immigration of needed skills. There are some restrictions - such as not being allowed to change jobs within three years of arrival - but the job market for computer staff is pretty buoyant.

Of course, all this assumes that you are white. If not, do not even consider South Africa.

Educational Requirements

The immigration department controls which skills are needed at any time. Computer skills are normally in demand.

Major Urban Centres

Johannesburg is the largest city in the country with a population of two million people - it is the industrial and commercial centre.

Other important cities are Pretoria, Capetown and Bloemfontein.

Major Industries

Mining is a major industry due to South Africa's immense wealth in minerals. It also has a thriving agricultural industry and manufacturing industry.

Economic Prospects

Although South Africa has suffered a relative decline recently, the underlying economy is very strong, because of its mineral wealth.

The political situation, though thorny, is by no means out of control, and it is unlikely that this will change much in the near future. The whites are well entrenched, and also beginning to make some of the right noises towards the blacks. Perhaps the whole country will peacefully turn the corner in the next century.

Educational System

There are plenty of excellent schools. All pupils must learn Afrikaans. Moreover, the political atmosphere is such that you should try to find a reasonably liberal school if your views do not tally with the white minority.

Travel

South Africa is better served with its transport system than most African countries. Its road network is comprehensive and speed restrictions should be observed. However, it does have one of the highest accident rates in the world.

There are also good air and rail links to most of the major cities.

CHAPTER 6

WORKING IN
THE FAR EAST
AND AUSTRALASIA

The Pacific Rim, embracing the Far Eastern countries, the American Western Seaboard and Australasia, is probably the area which will experience the most growth in the next century. The economic miracle of the Japanese economy, Taiwan and Korea are all signs of this. Californians now talk far more of their Pacific Rim connections than the older markets in the USA. Australia is undergoing a huge growth in confidence - although this has been somewhat muted by a few spectacular business failures.

The Far Eastern countries offer varying degrees of opportunity to the expatriate worker. The largest, Japan, was almost not included in this survey, largely because there are very few openings for westerners, except in multinational subsidiaries.

The Far East probably has more contrasts in peoples than anywhere else in the world. The oriental countries have a very distinct feel to them. Their way of doing business is very aggressive and they are proving the real economic dynamo at the end of the twentieth century.

Australasia might seem at first sight to be merely ex-colonial, in the European mould. Because of the populations of the countries, this is somewhat true. However, Australia particularly is becoming a country with a very distinct personality of its own.

HONG KONG

Introduction

Hong Kong is a small group of islands and a bit of the coast of mainland China. It is a Crown colony (almost the only one left), still administered by a British Governor. It came under British control after the Opium Wars in the nineteenth century. The peace terms under the Treaty of Nanking stated that the British should have a trading post. After much debate, the position of this post was fixed as the Kowloon peninsula, which was handed over in 1898 on a 99 year lease. Apart from the four years in the Second World War when the territory was occupied by the Japanese, the British have been in control throughout that time. However, the lease expires in 1997, and the British government signed an agreement in 1984 to hand the territory back in that year.

The terms of that agreement will, in theory, give Hong Kong special status enabling them to continue to operate as a capitalist haven within the communist state. However, since the massacre at Tianenmen Square in 1989, there have been well justified worries about the final outcome for the colony.

Meanwhile, Hong Kong remains a powerful financial force in the Far East, and a haven for much international business. It is one of the world's great banking centres, and the third financial centre after London and New York. There is also a lot of manufacturing - far more than its size would lead one to expect.

Opportunities in the Computer Industry

The opportunities available are almost all with subsidiary companies, normally in the banking and business fields.

Language(s) Spoken

Cantonese, and English for business.

Currency

The Hong Kong dollar (HK$) stands at HK$15 to the pound.

Cost of Living

The colony is not cheap - largely because of its remoteness, and the cost of apartments. You need to be earning at least 50 per cent more than in England. However, such salaries are not abnormal.

Local Taxation

Income tax is levied on an increasing scale, but is far lower than in the UK. There is no control on the repatriation of money.

Housing

The big problem in this overcrowded area. The guide price for a typical large flat is $25,000.

Other Job Opportunities

There are opportunities with subsidiaries of multinationals.

Work Permits

There are restrictions on expatriates taking jobs in Hong Kong, if these can be taken by local personnel. Most expatriates work for subsidiaries of multinational companies, or for the British government.

Educational Requirements

Because of the high level of literacy in Hong Kong, foreigners must be even more capable to be considered.

Major Urban Areas

Hong Kong Central is a thriving densely populated area as is Kowloon.

Major Industries

Hong Kong exudes energy - it is a major banking and insurance centre. The textiles and clothing industry is important as are the plastics and electronics industries and some heavy industry such as steel and iron.

Economic Prospects

It is hard to see beyond 1997. The Chinese claim that they will stick to their agreements, but after Tianenmen Square many people feel their word can hardly be trusted. There are plenty of people in Hong Kong who want to see the place continue to thrive, and one can only hope that this will be possible.

Educational System

There are English schools in the colony, and expatriates often send their children to boarding schools at home.

Travel

Hong Kong has a plentiful supply of a variety of different modes of transport - which is fortunate considering the massive number of people who use public transport. Methods of transport include buses, taxis, minibuses, the subway and on foot.

Driving is more problematic due to the lack of parking spaces. The main airport, Kai Tak airport is one of the busiest in the world.

JAPAN

Introduction

We all know about the Japanese miracle. By a careful mixture of setting long term objectives, co-operative management, the closing of borders to imported goods and plain hard work, the Japanese have made themselves dominant in many manufacturing areas.

This mountainous, volcanic country is composed of a number of islands, the largest of which is Honshu. Its population is huge - 123 million people pack the shores of the islands whose total area is just slightly less than Norway's. As a result the towns are terribly densely packed with people.

Japan has had a fairly chequered history. It was ruled by feudal barons until the end of the sixteenth century. However, threatened from the sea as it was, it managed to establish a reasonably united front for three hundred years before that. From 1600 to 1868 - the Tokugawa period - a monarchy was established, with a 'shogun' or emperor in overall charge. The country kept itself clear of outside influences in this period (shogun means 'Repeller of Barbarians', and that is what they did).

After 1868, the country began a very quick modernisation and industrialisation programme. At the same time, in line with many other powerful countries at the time, Japan began to try to establish an Empire, occupying Korea in 1905 after defeating the Russians.

In the 1920s and 1930s, Japan went after China, and in the process found themselves up against the British. This enmity caused them to declare themselves on Germany's side during World War Two.

The Japanese were able to drive through China and South-East Asia in the early years, pushing the British out of Singapore, Malaysia and Hong Kong. However, their luck changed with American involvement - brought about by the Japanese attack on Pearl Harbour in 1941. They were pushed back out of the islands, towards their final defeat after the nuclear bombing of Hiroshima and Nagasaki. Japan was then occupied by the Americans, who imposed the new constitutional government which they enjoy to this day.

Opportunities in the Computer Industry

There are many computers in Japan, but also many Japanese able to use them.

The Japanese attitude to foreigners is still fairly chauvinistic, and there are not many opportunities for expatriates, except those with foreign companies.

Language(s) Spoken

Japanese predominates, but the American influence has also led to some English being spoken.

Currency

The Japanese yen stood at 250.25 to the pound in early 1991.

Cost of Living

Very high - Tokyo is the most expensive city in the world. You need to earn a very much higher salary than your equivalent in the UK.

Local Taxation

Very complex. Expatriates only pay tax on income earned in Japan. Top rate taxation is 70 per cent. It must be taken into account that the transferring of Japanese money to the UK is not easy.

Housing

Expensive and hard to find.

Other Job Opportunities

Wives are unlikely to find work - the Japanese have a chauvinistic attitude towards 'the little woman'.

Work Permits

Up to six months may be spent without a visa, although a working visa is needed if you have a job there. They do not allow temporary (contract) workers.

Educational Requirements

None specifically - you will need to be pretty competent to compete with the local talent.

Major Urban Areas

Tokyo, the capital, is the nation's political and financial centre. Osaka is the commercial and industrial centre of western Japan.

Major Industries

Japanese industry is admired all over the world. It is the leading player in the electronics industry. Important companies include NEC, Hitachi, Matsushita and Fujitsu.

Economic Prospects

The economy has grown and grown. However, the Japanese stock market has recently been badly clobbered by the problems in the Gulf - it was very up and down before that.

The country seems to be entering the second stage of economic growth - when profits start to level off, and other, hungrier countries begin to emerge to threaten its dominance. However, it has also begun to diversify its manufacturing (Britain has been a major recipient of Japanese manufacturing investment) and looks set to remain one of the top economies in the world.

Educational System

Although there are a number of English speaking schools, the majority of British expatriates send their children to English boarding schools.

Travel

Japan has one of the most efficient railways with frequent services on all the main routes - 20,000 trains operate daily. Roads are narrow and crowded with slow traffic and with the additional problem of Japanese road signs which make driving yourself around difficult.

MALAYSIA

Introduction

The Federation of Malaysia consists of 13 states, of which 11 are on the mainland peninsular (the old state of Malaya, without Singapore) and the other two, Sarawak and Sabah are on an island, above Borneo. Much of the country is very swampy, and hot - the bottom of Sarawak is just above the equator.

The country was a British colony from the nineteenth century. It fell to a very rapid and surprising Japanese advance in the Second World War, which saw the fall of Singapore, considered impregnable, by troops who came overland through the peninsula.

The British took control again after the war, and created the Federation of Malaya, which, after a lot of bloodshed, became an independent country in 1957. In 1963, this merged with Singapore, and Sabah and Sarawak to form the Federation of Malaysia. Singapore seceded in 1965.

The population of Malaysia is a mixture of Malays (54 per cent), Chinese (35 per cent) and Indians (10 per cent). This still causes a lot of strife between the races.

The country is moving heavily into manufacturing, and some opportunities exist in that area for computer personnel.

Opportunities in the Computer Industry

Opportunities may exist with multinational offices. The fact that English is in widespread use is a benefit to British personnel.

Language(s) Spoken

The official language is Bahasa Malaysia - but English is widely spoken.

Currency

The Malaysian ringgitt is also known as the Malaysian Dollar. It stood at M$5.25 to the pound in early 1991.

Cost of Living

The cost of living is generally higher than in the UK, but not by a large margin.

Local Taxation

Income taxes are levied on Malaysian income and benefits in kind, on a pay as you earn basis. Tax rates vary from around 30 per cent to 45 per cent.

Housing

Accommodation is relatively easy to find, and an expatriate will normally have a house provided as part of the contract. A guide price for a house is around M$5000 per month in Kuala Lumpur. Cheaper housing is available further out.

Other Job Opportunities

There are some - although secretarial posts will be hard to find. There are also some controls on dependents finding work - they must apply to the authorities for permission.

Work Permits

A work permit is needed before you enter the country, and this must be provided by your prospective employer.

Educational Requirements

There are none specified.

Major Urban Centres

Kuala Lumpur is the capital with a one million population. It is a major commercial centre serving an important tin-mining and rubber-growing area.

Major Industries

The manufacturing industry is rapidly expanding. Malaysia is the number one country for semiconductor assembly in the world. The agricultural industry remains very important.

Economic Prospects

Like a number of other Pacific Rim countries, Malaysia is expanding its manufacturing capacity, alongside its traditional agricultural economy. It is also a petroleum producer.

Educational System

Most expatriates will send their children back to England for education.

Travel

Malaysian roads are among the best in South-East Asia and long distance express coaches cover most of the country. The trains, run by Malayan Railways, are comfortable and fares are reasonable.

SINGAPORE

Introduction

Singapore is at the point of the Malay peninsula. It is a little like Hong Kong. It became a crown colony in 1867. It was renowned as an impregnable fortress, and the last bastion of the British Far Eastern Empire. Indeed it was impregnable - to any invader who co-operated by coming in by sea. Unfortunately, in 1941, the Japanese came in by land, through the peninsula, and dealt a huge blow to British morale.

The country was freed after the war, and became self-governing in 1957. It amalgamated with Malaysia in 1963, but broke away again in 1965, since when it has been independent.

Although small, it has a natural harbour - one of the main reasons for the British presence, and second only in size to Rotterdam. This has given it a strong base in the entrepot trade (warehousing and import/export), shipbuilding, oil refining, and banking.

Opportunities in the Computer Industry

Because of the large numbers of expatriates in Singapore (a relic, perhaps of the days of Empire), there are opportunities, mainly in the business centres. Most jobs will be contracts rather than permanent jobs.

Language(s) Spoken

English is widely spoken, in addition Malay, Tamil and a number of other Chinese dialects are also spoken.

Currency

The Singapore dollar stood at S$3.35 to the pound in 1991.

Cost of Living

The cost of living is fairly low. Accommodation is not expensive, and the country is self-sufficient in some foods - although others, and more importantly some water, need to be imported. The per capita income in Singapore is second only to that in Japan.

Local Taxation

Tax is due on money earned in Singapore and on some benefits in kind on a progressive scale up to 40 per cent. Short term residents pay different rates, depending on the length of stay.

Housing

Reasonably available. A guide price for a three-bedroomed apartment is S$2500 per month.

Other Job Opportunities

There are opportunities for spouses, but a separate work permit will be needed.

Work Permits

The employer must apply for an employment or a professional visit pass. They will also need to apply for you to bring in your family.

Educational Requirements

Normal skill levels.

Major Urban Centres

Singapore, with a population of one million people, is the capital and most important city.

Major Industries

Entrepot trade, oil refining, banking and shipbuilding are all vital industries.

Economic Prospects

The joining of Hong Kong to China in 1997 is bringing quite a lot of business to Singapore, as companies move the bulk of their operations to a more stable environment. The position of the country also makes it a natural communications hub.

Educational System

There are English private schools, and many expatriates send their children home to boarding schools.

Travel

Singapore is only 224 square miles wide and a comprehensive road network exists, which makes it easy to get around. There is also a railway which goes all the way around the island and links it to Thailand and Malaysia.

AUSTRALIA

Introduction

Australia is a huge and beautiful continent, with a very low population, mainly of English-speaking people, although there are pockets of other Europeans and orientals.

Australia's history as a colony dates back more than 200 years - almost as long as America has been independent. However, its development has been far more along colonial lines, and its system of government is closer to Britain's. The Queen is the constitutional head of government.

The country was known as early as 1606 to the Dutch East India Company, which established a settlement on the north west coast, which they called New Holland. The Eastern Seaboard was mapped and opened up by Captain Cook in the late eighteenth century.

Britain, stung by the loss of its American colonies in 1776, decided to use Australia as a prison colony, rather than building up a substantial population of settlers who might turn against the Crown. The transportation of prisoners went on until 1868, and by that time more than 150,000 prisoners had been sent there.

The discovery of gold started a rush of immigrants, eager to make themselves rich. Their displacement of the native aborigines was as depressing as the spread of 'civilised' man to other continents. However, the aboriginal population, now reduced, is hanging on.

Despite its huge size, Australia's population is largely concentrated in the cities, which are all coastal. Inland, there are settlements, but the majority of the continent is still wilderness.

The Australian cities vary very much in style, and an immigrant can almost choose the type, from semi-tropical Darwin through cosmopolitan Sydney to the more European Adelaide.

Opportunities in the Computer Industry

The computer scene is very similar to that in the UK, dominated by IBM, with some DEC and the others. Few ICL trained analysts will find work in Australia where there are few ICL machines. As usual IBM provides the coveted standard, with DB2 skills in high demand. Adabus and Natural are both popular languages, while a quick survey of *Australian Computerworld* reveals that AS/400 and System 38 are two of the most marketable skills. This probably reflects the fact that the average size of company is somewhat smaller than in the UK.

Melbourne, Sydney and Canberra all offer data processing jobs but Perth has the highest number of UK immigrants attracted by the inexpensive yet luxurious standard of living. Employers include major banks, insurance, manufacturing and oil companies such as BP and Shell.

Even though salaries are higher, it would be a great mistake to assume that working in Australia would make you richer. As most salary or tax bonuses are mopped up by higher prices and taxes, the real enrichment is in the quality of life. The improvements in the quality of life includes cheaper leisure pursuits.

At the time of writing this, the Australian market for overseas IT personnel is deflated due to the weak state of the economy. Therefore the contracting market is very small and so opportunities in anything but the most in demand skills are quite scarce.

Language(s) Spoken

The Australian version of English is familiar to us all from television advertisements.

Currency

The Australian dollar stood at A$2.45 at the beginning of 1991.

Cost of Living

The locally produced foodstuffs are very cheap and abundant. However, manufactured goods are expensive, often as much as twice their price in Britain. Many immigrants take electrical appliances with them - but you should be aware of the differences in voltage (there are 220 volt and 110 volt outlets), and the television system is slightly different. Cars are well worth exporting, as long as you make sure that they are up to Australian safety standards.

Local Taxation

Income tax is progressive, on a pay as you earn basis, up to a maximum of 49 per cent. There are also sales taxes on some goods. In addition, the Australian health insurance scheme, Medicare, is paid for by contributions from salary, up to a limit. This pays for 85 per cent of the fees which are due for medical treatment. This can be applied to private treatment as well as state provided, however the limit is 85 per cent of the amount deemed correct under the state system.

Housing

Accommodation is relatively easy - although it varies by city (Sydney is probably the most difficult). A guide price for a three-bedroomed apartment is A$800 per month. Purchasing property is a good option if you are emigrating,as it is, on the whole, far cheaper than in Britain, although Australian interest rates have been at similar high levels to our own recently.

Other Job Opportunities

There are reasonably good job opportunities generally in the towns.

Work Permits

Australia has a quota system for immigration, based upon 126,000 entrants per year. Assessing the suitability of candidates is done by a complex quota system, based on four components - family, skill, special eligibility and humanitarianism. Points gained in the assessment detailed below go to make up a passmark, which implies that the candidate is fit to settle. However, after that comes an interview with a member of the Australian Government. This points systems applies to the 'concessional' category of 'family migration' (where you have Australian relatives to sponsor you), or the 'independent' category of 'skill migration'.

Applicants under the concessional family category can score points under skill, age, relationship, citizenship, settlement and location. Under the independent skills section, points are scored under skill, age and language ability. If you and your partner are both qualified, only one person's qualifications are taken into account.

The tables are too complex to list here, and the points change from time to time. An 'application for a migration kit' is available from the Australian Embassy for a charge of A$5. Some agencies which specialise in Australian work will arrange the assessment for you.

Educational Requirements

The point system naturally favours those with a degree or a diploma qualification. Computer skills are normally in demand.

Major Urban Centres

Australia's population is centred upon a number of cities vast distances away from each other. Sydney, situated on the east coast, is Australia's largest city. Perth, with a population of one million people, is western Australia's primary city. Brisbane and Melbourne are also major cities.

Major Industries

Australia is a well-resourced country with a wide industrial base. Agriculture is also important as are the engineering, food processing and oil refining industries.

Economic Prospects

Australia has good prospects. It has suffered somewhat recently from a series of company failures, such as the crash of the Bond company, and it has had to contend with high interest rates and low growth. However, it is a very well stocked country and has good prospects.

Educational System

The education system is free but private schools are also available.

Travel

As Australia is such a vast country the only realistic way to travel between cities is by flying. The rail network is limited and mainly based only in the east of the country.

All the main cities have good internal road links but beware once you leave the main highways since some of the roads are just dust tracks.

NEW ZEALAND

Introduction

New Zealand is quite a large country - just slightly larger than the United Kingdom - with a largely agricultural economy. It is very beautiful, and very much like home to its largely British descended population. It is split into two islands, and the majority of its population live in the North Island.

The country was settled by Polynesian Maoris over 1000 years ago. As with Australia, though, it was Captain Cook who did the first exploration and mapping. The British colonised the island, and it became a dominion in 1907. Like Australia, its head of state is the Queen, and it has a democratically elected government. This came to the world stage in the mid-1980s, when the Labour Party under David Lange took control. They were fiercely anti-nuclear, and banned nuclear powered ships, or those carrying atomic weapons, from entering the country's waters. In a pretty blatant act of piracy, the Greenpeace ship, *Rainbow Warrior*, in the area to protest against the French use of Pacific Atolls for nuclear tests, was sunk by a French team of saboteurs. This, and the government attitude on nuclear power, brought the country into world focus.

The economy is largely agricultural, although there is some manufacturing. However, this is largely cottage industry stuff - firms with 10 or less employees.

To a city dweller, New Zealand will seem pretty frumpy and uninteresting. If you like outdoor life, it is wonderful.

Opportunities in the Computer Industry

There are not that many computer installations in New Zealand, but there are opportunities, and computer personnel are needed, particularly for smaller machines.

Similarly to Australia, the New Zealand economy is at the moment in a slump, so opportunities for overseas IT personnel are more scarce than in more buoyant times.

Language(s) Spoken

English and Maori (spoken by the Maori people).

Currency

The New Zealand dollar stood at NZ$3.24 to the pound in early 1991.

Cost of Living

The cost of living is fairly similar to that in the UK, although manufactured goods like cars are particularly expensive.

Local Taxation

Progressive to a maximum rate of 48 per cent, with a 'goods and services' tax (similar to VAT) of ten per cent.

Housing

Most New Zealanders live in bungalows, which are mainly purchased. There is little rented accommodation available.

Other Job Opportunities

There are some in the cities - but your spouse must share your love of the outdoor life.

Work Permits

The country operates a system called the Occupational Priority List (OPL), which includes computer personnel. They must have a professional qualification and/or relevant experience, along with a job offer for a salary of not less than NZ$ 28,000 p.a. (this has been the case since September 1989).

Educational Requirements

A professional qualification and/or relevant experience are necessary to get a computer job.

Major Urban Centres

Auckland is New Zealand's largest city and also its fastest growing. Other major areas are Wellington, the capital, and Christchurch, the main city on the South Island.

Major Industries

The most important industry is agriculture; there is also some manufacturing although this is mostly on a small scale.

Economic Prospects

The country is not exactly bubbling with growth, and has a high rate of inflation. However, it meanders along reasonably successfully, and there's always the great outdoors.

Educational System

There is a pretty good education system. Out of the cities, the classes are very small, and children are well looked after. There are also private schools available.

Travel

New Zealand has a comprehensive network of road, rail, sea and air transportation. Highways are of a high standard. An International Driving Licence is required if you wish to drive.

Probably to your advantage, driving is the on the left-hand side of the road.

CHAPTER 7

WORKING IN NORTH AMERICA

The North American continent is, in many ways, the most attractive place for British workers. Not only is the language not a problem (except in French Canada), but also the standard of living is generally higher. However, it is easy to spend far more over there, because of the greater range of leisure and social activities normally on offer.

The computer industry is rooted in the USA, and that marketplace is certain to be attractive. However, it is not as easy to move there as you might imagine, since the US authorities are trying to restrict immigration to those with skills which cannot be found indigenously. Because of the usual shortage of computer skills, you could be luckier than others in finding work there, but permanent residence may still be denied to you.

Canada is a rather simpler exercise. Although they, too, are restricting entry, those with computer skills should not have much trouble getting in.

CANADA

Introduction

Canada occupies a slightly larger area than the USA - making it second in land area only to the USSR - but it has roughly a tenth of the population. However, a lot of that land is barren and arctic.

Canadians are proud of not being American. Their constitution is a monarchy, headed by the Queen, with a two tier parliament.

Canada is split into ten provinces, each with its own Lieutenant General and an elected legislature. There are also two territories, constituted by acts of Parliament. The province of Quebec is fiercely adamant that it should use the French language - there are many who would like to see it as a separate country.

Canada remained British after the American War of Independence. In 1791, the Canada Act was passed, which split the country into regions. These more or less corresponded with the older French-speaking parts, and the newer British. Each region had its own legislative council. However, this was a failure, and the whole country became one as a dominion in the mid-1800s.

Canada has been a very loyal subject nation to the British crown, and Canadians have always rallied to help Britain in times of need. As a result, the Canadians have not been keen to be identified with the United States - although their borders are fairly open. Despite these perceived differences, Canadians have much more in common with Americans than with British (they even play baseball and American football).

Their relationship with the USA is changing somewhat, since their government, under Brian Mulroney, has identified the United States of America as an important trading partner.

Opportunities in the Computer Industry

Canada has a well developed computer market, and a number of major corporations which are very significant users. There are good opportunities there for suitably qualified people. However, as with most countries, their entry requirements are becoming stricter.

Language(s) Spoken

Although the major language is English, there are many French speakers in and around the province of Quebec.

Currency

The Canadian dollar stood at C$2.25 to the pound in early 1991.

Cost of Living

Canada has a fairly average cost of living. It is higher than that in the USA, mainly because of the harsher climate plus the higher heating bills, etc.

Local Taxation

Tax is deducted on a pay as you earn basis, but, as in the USA, you make an annual tax return. Tax rates are progressive, and there are a number of allowances available. If you are a resident, you are expected to pay taxes on all income from any source, and federal and local taxes are levied.

Sales taxes are also payable, using a VAT type of system.

Housing

Housing can be expensive. The guide price for a three-roomed apartment is $1000 per month. This should include heating - a major cost item in such a cold climate.

Other Job Opportunities

There are reasonable opportunities in the cities.

Work Permits

Immigration is based on the principle of non-discrimination. The government tries to select immigrants who will enrich Canadian life and be able to fit into the population. Visas will be granted if accompanied by an application from an employer. Therefore you must obtain a work permit before entering the country. There is a 'hire Canadian first' policy in force, but the country has a relatively relaxed attitude to immigration and expatriates particularly where there are skill shortages.

For government jobs (if there is no suitable native person to fill the post) you need to have a working knowledge of French, since most communications are in both languages.

Educational Requirements

Skilled workers need to be able to prove qualifications, but this is not as rigorous as for the USA or Australia.

Major Urban Centres

Canada's main cities are Toronto, Montreal and Vancouver.

Montreal is an important industrial port. Toronto, Canada's largest city with a population of three million, is likewise a major commercial and industrial port. Vancouver is the commercial and industrial base of British Columbia.

Major Industries

Canada has rich natural resources, so has important industries in mining, forestry and oil. Agriculture, especially wheat growing, is another major industry.

Canada has also got a firm manufacturing base, despite its current problems, and is the sixth ranking manufacturing and trading nation in the world.

Economic Prospects

Canada has abundant oil and mineral reserves - and its economy suffered from the pre-Gulf crisis falls in oil prices. The general outlook is, however, relatively pessimistic since Canadian performance is tied to that in the USA. The manufacturing sector is particularly weak at the moment because of high interest rates.

Educational System

The education system is not dissimilar to that in Britain, although in Quebec the language spoken is French. There are some private schools, but generally schooling is free. The Canadians have implemented a student loans scheme for university students.

Travel

As Canada is such a vast country the most feasible way to travel between major cities is by air. If you have plenty of time, there are several long distance coach services which can take you anywhere in the country.

Within the main towns, the transport systems are well-equipped with extensive bus and train services. Road conditions out of the towns can be harsh during the cold winters.

UNITED STATES OF AMERICA

Introduction

In many ways, this seems the easiest country to introduce, because we are so familiar with it through the movies, music and television. However, America is a gigantic country which embraces an enormous range of ethnic types, religions and backgrounds. It also covers a very wide range of climates, from tropical to arctic (if you include Alaska). In many ways the USA is a number of countries bound up together into one.

The American people are friendly and easy to work and socialise with. The American greeting 'have a nice day' is often criticised in Europe. However, this is very unfair. At least it is said, and sometimes with conviction. The wish to be friendly is definitely there. If you enter a lift (elevator), and find other people there, they will normally greet you. This degree of friendliness may be quite disconcerting but is well meant and very attractive.

American society which, whilst it may be rooted in Europe, is markedly different. Their culture is based upon a greater geographical insularity than Europe's, because of the size of the country. There are still many Americans who have never been abroad and have a very vague idea of the structure of the rest of the world.

The American marketplace is vast. There are many major centres which are as large as or larger than any in Europe. Moreover, the fact that all this is one country means that it is possible to work on a countrywide basis.

Choosing to live or work in America will involve not only the choice of company, but also the choice of city. With such a vast landmass, you can decide this taking into account the climate, ethnic or religious background, type of people (from city dwelling sophisticate to hill billy) and many other factors. If you have no particular set of requirements in mind, it is as well to do some research on what is available.

Geographically, a lot of America is undeveloped - 70 per cent of its people live in the cities. The countryside includes every conceivable type of land from huge tracts of the most fertile farmlands to scrub, from blazing deserts to alpine mountains. It is a country capable of surprising you for a lifetime with its enormous variety of beauty.

America is split into states which are partly autonomous, with a governor, senate and house of representatives. They may enact legislation and raise taxes over and above the federal level. The federal government in Washington is responsible for national issues - defence, foreign policy and overall monetary affairs.

There are large differences in prosperity from one region to another. At one time, for instance, the East Coast was the most affluent, along with California. However, the recession in manufacturing, and the growth of the Pacific Rim has changed that. Now cities like Seattle - once little more than a backwater - are far more prosperous than the old 'patrician' cities like Boston. As a result, costs - particularly of property - can vary enormously from area to area.

Although America was once a colony, it is very far away from that now. People who have not been there tend to think of it as all new and brash. However, this is not true. The country has been settled in for many years, and its architecture, for instance, though distinctive, is often no newer than that in major cities in Europe - most of which were extensively built up only in the last 100 years. It is not the 'new' world any more, except where it is still under development.

The USA is an established, solid country, with as much tradition as most others - even though it cannot trace its roots back as far. Moreover, although Americans may seek their individual roots, they are proud of being American, and will, in general, only see their previous ancestry as being of general interest. An American born an Englishman will usually be as American as any other.

Opportunities in the Computer Industry

The size and scope of the country means that potential opportunities are almost endless, in all possible spheres - as long as you can satisfy the entry requirements. California and especially Silicon Valley have always be seen to be the spiritual home of computing, but there are opportunities in many different states.

At the present time, opportunities are more limited than in previous years due to the slump in the US economy. Contracts also do not appear quite as attractive as before because of the poor dollar-pound exchange rate. As the higher salaries or tax bonuses tend to be mopped up by higher prices, it is the quality of life which often persuades people to work in the USA. Leisure activities are cheaper in America.

One microcode specialist, who moved to the US with his company, is earning around $50,000 a year, which is about £10,000 more than with the same company in the UK. But he feels that the elasticity of his money is about the same as in the UK. Expensive housing (in his case San Francisco) is eating away the increase in salary. But he is confident that his real enrichment was in the quality of life. Leisure activities particularly are cheaper.

Contracts tend to be at least a year's duration and salary reflect the local marketplace.

Similarly to the UK marketplace, the skills which are most in demand include C, Unix, Tandem and DB2. It is in these areas that higher salaries can be commanded.

The main employers of foreign IT staff are the mainstream commercial companies such as banks, insurance companies and airlines.

Language(s) Spoken

Although English is the main language, Spanish is very common in the South. The American version of English is a very vibrant language with many dialects. Words used in New York, for instance, may be quite different from those in California.

Currency

The American dollar stood at $1.95 to the pound in early 1991.

Cost of Living

The cost of living varies greatly. In the plusher cities, it may be very much greater than in the UK, but out of town it can be markedly lower. Costs are generally lower, but there is a lot more to spend your money on, so it may not appear to go so far.

Local Taxation

Federal taxes are levied on income on an incremental scale. Every citizen must make a tax return each year, and the form is far more complex than its British equivalent. There are now less allowances to claim than previously.

The American pay as you earn system is less complex than ours, and less efficient. Because of this most citizens' tax returns will yield a rebate or extra tax.

The rates of income tax are lower in the USA (15 and 28 per cent), but there are additional taxes to the state and even the town. These state taxes may be levied on income and on sales. You pay state income tax in the state in which you work, sales tax on the goods at the place in which you buy the goods.

Sales taxes can be very confusing, since you may have more than one tax to pay on a purchase (state and local). The Americans have not managed any better than we have to produce a good local taxation system - but it is up to the town or state to decide which to adopt. It can be a surprise to cross a state line and find the same goods costing far more, or far less, because of a different set of sales taxes.

Housing

You cannot generalise - some towns are much cheaper, some much more expensive. Housing in California is very expensive, with a studio flat in San Francisco starting at around $900 in rent a month, and an average family home costing about $300,000, although in other places it is much cheaper.

In some cities, like New York, the majority of people live in apartments, in others, such as Seattle, they live in houses. Even architectural styles vary wildly across the continent.

Other Job Opportunities

There are many job opportunities - but visa requirements may make it hard for a partner to work. The wife of a friend of mine who is a university professor went to find a job for herself on the campus. She holds a doctorate in English Literature, and was amused, and slightly insulted, to be told that she would need a literacy test, as a foreigner, before she could work as a teacher there. She did get the job, of course.

Work Permits

The situation with regards to work permits is complex, and basically divides into whether you want to apply to immigrate or not.

If you wish to immigrate, there is an overall annual limit of 270,000 people imposed, of which 20,000 may be from any one country.

There are six 'preference categories' for immigration, who will make up a proportion of the total number of immigrants.

- Category one is the unmarried sons and daughters, over 21, of US citizens. This represents 20 per cent of the 270,000 limit.

- Category two is the spouses and unmarried children of aliens being admitted for permanent residence. This represents 26 per cent of the 270,000 limit.

- Category three is the members of professions or exceptional persons who will substantially benefit the US economy, cultural interest or welfare, and are sought after by an employer in the USA. This represents ten per cent of the 270,000 limit.

- Category four is the married children over 21 of US citizens - ten per cent of the limit.

- Category five is the brothers and sisters of US citizens over 21. This represents 24 per cent of the 270,000 limit.

- Category six is those with necessary skills which it can be proved cannot be fulfilled from the US labour pool. This represents ten per cent of the 270,000.

Those applying to be allowed into the US in categories three and six must get certification from the US Department of Labor, to ensure that the immigrant will not displace a native worker, or adversely affect wages and conditions of similarly employed US workers. The employer has a duty to show that he or she has tried unsuccessfully to recruit for the post in the USA. There is a committee to vet such applications. The process can take six months to a year to satisfy requirements. The date of acceptance then establishes the individual's priority position against the numerical limitation system.

In addition, 'Schedule A' classification can be used to bypass this process in the following classes:

Group I - physiotherapists, physicians in certain areas; Group II - exceptional ability in sciences or arts (excluding performing arts), including college teachers; Group III - religious workers; Group IV - international business executives and managers. To earn this classification needs lots of paperwork.

If you are a non-immigrant, there are a number of different visa types:

Type B is temporary for business or pleasure. This is the normal American visa. It is theoretically not necessary now to have a visa when entering America for a holiday or brief business trip. However, American immigration workers are not all familiar with the change, and it is wise to apply for one anyway - you are unlikely to be refused. B-1 visas are solely for business, B-2 solely for pleasure. These visas are not intended for study or performing of skilled or unskilled labour, as opposed to conducting business on behalf of foreign employer. A stay may last for one year, but normally only for six months.

Type E is for treaty traders - those carrying on business in US solely to develop and direct operations of enterprise between US and treaty state. These normally involve you in proving that you are going to invest a substantial sum in the enterprise.

Type I is for representatives of the information media, who must have evidence of their intent eventually to leave the country. They run for one year initially, and can be extended by one year repeatedly. The worker can be accompanied by a spouse and children. It is necessary to prove that the holder is coming as the representative of foreign media solely to engage in that vocation. Once granted, the holder may only change employer and retain the visa with approval from the US immigration service.

Type J is for exchange scholars.

Type H are the visas for temporary workers.

Type H-1 is for professionals, who must show that their talents are needed. The must have at least a degree or be able to show sufficient professional experience, or pre-eminence in a field, to warrant the granting of such a visa. They last for up to two years, during which time, the holder must continue to work with a particular employer. If the employer can then show a continuing need, the visa can be extended by one year increments. A new petition is needed if the employer changes.

Type H-2 is for those in the medical profession (not students).

Type H-3 is for trainees entering the country purely to undergo training.

The last category is L-1 is for inter-company transfers for managers or specialists. They must have been continuously employed by the company abroad for more than one year. The job must be the same in the US as at home and they must depart when it is complete. In addition, the company must be able to show that this person will enable it to be more competitive and/or open new markets. Blanket petitions can be filed to move a team of employees over. The visa may be applicable for up to three years - however, local immigration offices may restrict this to one year.

The result of all this is that if you are intending to emigrate, you may have a very long wait. Merely obtaining a job is not enough, nor even is qualifying. You must literally wait for your number to come up. The United States is a huge country, but it also has a large and growing population. Such restrictions are considered necessary to control the increase.

Educational Requirements

The educational requirements are pretty well laid out in the previous section. Broadly speaking, you must have at least a degree to be considered - although you may be accepted on the basis of your professional expertise.

On the East Coast of America more emphasis is put on having appropriate qualifications.

Major Urban Areas

The USA has a great number of important urban centres, the largest being New York - a vibrant centre of nearly eight million people.

Los Angeles is also vast with a population of over seven million. Other major cities include Denver, Dallas, Boston, Chicago and Seattle.

Major Industries

The US is such a major economy that many, different industries are of a massive scale and of worldwide importance. It also has one of the most important manufacturing bases, companies such as Ford, and has good natural mineral resources.

The US contests with Japan for the premier position in the electronics and computer industry; it is the home of IBM.

Finance and banking are also fundamental to the USA, as is the agriculture industry.

Economic Prospects

The US economy is enormously strong. If it fails, the world will suffer, as we have seen on a number of occasions. However, there are dark clouds on the horizon. Inflation and interest rates are higher than is comfortable. The Gulf Crisis added to the uncertainty. But over-riding all of this is the federal budget deficit.

The National Debt of America has doubled and doubled again in the last ten years. This situation is causing enormous worry, since there seems no simple way to cure the problem. President Bush has backed himself into a corner by promising no new taxes (although that does not necessarily imply no increase of current rates). We have recently had the spectacle of American national monuments being closed for a day because of lack of funds. However this is all resolved, the way will be bumpy.

Nonetheless, the American economy has so much inherent strength that it is unlikely to founder.

Educational System

The American system is comprehensive and of variable quality. In general terms literacy is not much better than ours. However, there are pockets of both excellence and poorness.

Boarding and private schools are often run on English public school lines - their fees are also at similarly inflated levels.

Remember that American society is very different from English, and the school curriculum reflects this. Some English parents are not too keen for their children to be brought up as Americans.

Travel

The USA has an excellent travel infrastructure. It is such a vast country that the quickest way to get around the country is by air. Rail and road networks are good. The freeway system covers all well populated areas.

Individual cities and towns have excellent internal transport systems.

CHAPTER 8

LOOKING AFTER YOUR FAMILY AND DEPENDANTS

It may seem obvious that, when contemplating moving abroad, you should discuss the matter carefully with any dependants or family. However, it is very easy to be caught up in a wave of enthusiasm and not to think of the effect that your decision might have on them.

If you have no immediate family, or partner, you are a prime candidate for working overseas. However, few people have absolutely no relatives. It has been very distressing to watch the reaction of parents and friends to the recent events in the Middle East. Single, unattached sons and daughters have been caught up in the conflict, and their relatives have been nervously watching the news to find out whether they are safe. In some cases the first news came from seeing the back of a head in a bus carrying escapees from Baghdad. The choice of workplace is important if such considerations may apply to you. Therefore, think of your family and friends, even though you may be independent of them.

PRESSURES ON YOUR PARTNER

If you have a partner, you will almost certainly discuss any decision with them. (To avoid appearing sexist by referring to the partner as the female or male, I will use the neuter form, 'they'). You may have a very exciting job ahead, but is there is no work work for them and they are used to working, it would be cruel to take them from that environment and force them to live at home out of contact with family and friends.

It is not always easy to obtain a work visa and your partner may be unable to get one even if you can get one with comparative ease. That is a pretty effective way to strain your relationship to breaking point.

Sexism

If you are male, and contemplating moving to a country where there is less equality for women, such as a middle eastern state, remember the effect that this may have on your partner. She may not be allowed to work at all, or to go out unaccompanied (or even to drive a car). The normal mores are suspended - women are often prevented from contact with men outside their own families. She might accept this situation, but you should very carefully investigate attitudes before making any commitment.

If you are female, similar considerations might apply. It is unlikely that you will choose to move to a country where you will have restrictions imposed upon you because of your sex - in the IT industry there are too many opportunities available without that kind of hassle. However, the local attitude may be rather different from that at home, and this can be unsettling for you or your partner. For instance, in America you may find that you are treated as more of an equal than in this country. That is a good thing - but how will your partner feel if you have to be out late regularly on company business? Such potential problems are far less severe for you than if you moved with your partner to a Muslim country - but can nevertheless strain a relationship.

Settling in a Different Country

An American friend of mine, who has settled in Germany, reckons that it is wrong to contemplate moving abroad after the age of 40, because by then you are established, and find it harder to accommodate the change.

Whether the magic number is accurate or not for you, there is no doubt that, as you grow older, you become less able or willing to change your habits. A move abroad might re-invigorate you, but equally it might leave you feeling very alone and depressed. Your partner, unless completely acquiescing in your decision, may feel even less happy with the move.

If your partner has to make a big upheaval to move with you - leaving a job, a set of friends and family - make sure that they have completely accepted the change, and are as enthusiastic about it as you are. If not, as the novelty wears off, you may find yourself having to buy a single ticket home for them - or having to move back yourself in an unplanned fashion.

WELFARE OF CHILDREN

If you have children, the problems are naturally even more complex. If you are paid well enough, you may be able to afford to send them to boarding schools in the UK. Multinational oil companies, and the services, for instance, often provide such services for their staff. However, if you want to keep the family together, you may want to find local schools for the children.

You will have to decide whether you want the children to go to a foreign school (in which the only language spoken may be foreign), or to an expatriate school. There are American schools in many countries, but remember that their educational system is different from the British, in style and syllabus.

You must ask yourself whether your children will need to return eventually to an English school. Now that we have a national curriculum, and the GCSE syllabus (which is a two or three year program incorporating coursework), can your children return and pass the necessary exams? You need to take into account their ages, and the length of stay which you are contemplating. If you intend to stay abroad permanently, this is not a problem - send them to local schools, and they will be able to mix completely with the local people.

The age of children is important. You might well be very successful in moving toddlers to a foreign language country. They will soon pick up a different language, and probably become bilingual. However, after a certain age, things are more difficult. Moving teenagers abroad, who have little language aptitude, can be problematic. Unsettling any child at that age can cause problems in their later lives. Of course, equally it can be a glorious and exciting game, and leave them stimulated in later life - and more able to accept changes than those brought up in a single country.

MAKING THE DECISION

Above all, remember that the decision does not entirely rest with you. However rosy your own prospects are, you may inadvertently inflict harm on those closest to you if you do not take them fully into account at the outset.

Do not underestimate how traumatic the move can be for both you and anyone you take with you - the culture shock can be greater than you imagine. But it is said by all those who have worked abroad or are still working abroad that the first few months abroad are the most difficult. If you and your family can survive these months without too much turmoil, then life becomes much easier.

CHAPTER 9

WORKING WITH AGENCIES

An important way to find an overseas post is via an agency specialising in that country. Although you may be able to find a job without such a contact, it is sensible to use an agency, and rely on their knowledge and experience.

Agencies in the computer business which specialise in overseas jobs tend to work in particular geographical areas. As a result, they will generally have local knowledge and be able to lead you through the minefield of work permits, finding accommodation and so on. See Appendix IV for a list of agencies specialising in finding IT work in other countries.

WORKING IN EUROPE

In Europe, because of the short distances involved, and the general mobility of labour, the agencies usually work very much like normal UK-only agents. If you are going to work in Europe, this may mean that you have to set up your own travel and accommodation arrangements. This might be rather difficult at a distance - particularly if you do not speak the language. Make sure that you know precisely what the agent will or will not do for you.

WORKING IN DISTANT COUNTRIES

Agents who arrange jobs further afield generally do more for you. If you are going to America, for instance, you should find that your agent will arrange for you to be met on arrival, and for your accommodation. Some larger agencies actually employ relocaters, who will seek out appropriate accommodation for you. The agent, or your prospective employer, should also arrange your visa.

In the USA it is also important that your credit rating is arranged for you before you arrive - most agencies and companies are able to make these arrangements for you or at least guide you in the right direction.

Australian agents should also help with calculating your points and making sure that a valid visa is in place before you leave your previous job.

If you are emigrating, you will probably be going to a permanent job. You will certainly be paid locally, and expect to become part of the new society. The situation is different if you are moving to a contract position abroad. American contracts, for instance, are often temporary.

The actual contract structure varies. In some cases you will be contracted to a local company, and local laws will apply. Make sure that you understand the implications of such contracts. It is very hard, for instance, to fight American companies, when their contract is written in a certain state, and you are languishing back in England.

WORKING IN THE MIDDLE EAST

Middle Eastern jobs are often on a temporary basis. Sometimes this means that you will be paid directly in the country, more often that you will receive at least a proportion abroad. Very often you will be paid 'second hand' by the agent, in the manner of most English contracts. There are some cautionary tales here. It is no secret that job agents - particularly those in the contracting marketplace - are in some difficulties these days.

The downturn in the economy has forced many to the wall, and left contractors with large amounts of money owing. A contractor abroad will have particular difficulty in this case, since he or she will be in a foreign, less understanding country with different laws and customs.

BAD EXPERIENCES

A contractor was hired in London to go and work in the Middle East. Even at the time of hiring, the agency knew that they were going to the wall, but, with a disregard for commonsense, they sent him anyway. The agreement was that they would receive money from the client, and pass it on, less their commission, to the contractor. Shortly after he arrived, with a wife and young child, the agency gave up the ghost. The contract was cancelled, and he was left without work in the foreign country.

He was lucky, in that he picked up another job relatively easily, and stayed there long enough to make his move worthwhile. He was naturally very bitter about the agency's actions.

Others, not in the computing field, have been less lucky. They have been deported, even imprisoned, because their work permits, which assumed a particular employer, were deficient.

Such experiences are the exceptions but nevertheless you must be made aware of this negative side. Most agencies are excellent at not only paying you on time but helping to organise housing and educational opportunites and more - their guidance will be invaluable to anyone moving overseas.

GOING DIRECT TO A CLIENT

Going direct with a client may seem a more attractive option. However, make sure that the client knows the ropes. If they have not employed contractors before, they may not know all the work permit requirements in their own country (how many British firms know all our regulations?). They might make you a firm offer, only to find that they cannot substantiate it because of bureaucratic problems. Normally the multinationals, and those used to moving staff around, like engineering companies, know what has to be done.

What do you *really* need to know about the world of overseas contracting?

 The last thing we want to do is spoil the excitement of working abroad. But we will take care of the rest. Visas, accommodation, tickets, schools... You could do the admin yourself, but wouldn't you rather just have the adventure – and enjoy the rewards?

Since 1972, Knight Programming Support Limited has been the first and foremost recruitment consultancy in international computing contracts. Our top priority is to find you the right opportunity – then sort out the details.

As part of BET, the specialist support services company, we have contacts throughout the industry. We also have the resources to guarantee prompt payment in full. Our network of offices throughout Europe and the USA is supported by a highly-qualified consultancy team based right here in the UK-so, not only can we find you the position you want, wherever you want, we'll also provide full support and advice, on the spot, for as long as your contract lasts.

Taking your skills overseas will be a standard feature of tomorrow's business world. Why not keep one jump ahead – with Knight Programming Support?

CHAPTER 10

DEALING WITH MOVING AND ACCOMMODATION

The most immediate questions when deciding to move overseas are what will you do with your current house and where will you live when you get to the foreign country. Every step you take must be carefully mapped out in financial terms.

RENTING OUT YOUR ACCOMMODATION

Clearly there are no simple answers, because every case will differ to some extent. If you intend to return to the UK eventually, you may not want to sell your home before you go. Therefore you need to find a tenant who will keep the house up and pay the expenses while you are away. Finding such tenants involves going to Estate Agents, and looking in the papers for 'long let' agencies.

Problems with Tenants

There can be problems with tenants. A musician I knew took a job in South Africa (hardly the most sensible choice in view of the Musicians Union's attitude to the country - it took him some time to re-establish himself over here). He let his house out before he went, arranging the tenancy privately with some nurses who wanted somewhere to live for about a year.

It was agreed that the nurses could 'rotate' - the actual tenants changing as long as the overall rent was still paid. A few months later, a new nurse moved in. She was unhappy with the price (even though it had all been acceptable to the original tenants, and a contract was in force). She decided to take the matter to the rent tribunal of the rather left-wing borough in which the house was situated. They reduced the rent - which they are able to do unilaterly.

The owner could not replace the tenants nor, at that distance, could he do very much to defend his position. He had to accept that now he was receiving less in rental than he was paying on his mortgage and other costs.

In a second case, a university lecturer went to work in America. Although his was a pretty permanent move (he has been there now for eight years), he decided to keep his flat in England as a 'bolt hole' in case anything went wrong. He rented the place out through a property company on a yearly basis. He managed to arrange that the house went to university students who would be there only during the academic year. This enabled him to make periodic trips home and stay in the house whilst there.

His problem was that the agent was so far away that it was very difficult to check up on what was happening. He had periods when tenants suddenly went missing and he lost money through that, and when they decided to stay during the vacation, he then could not use the house, and had to stay in the USA or with friends in England.

Another far more trivial problem was that he left his car in the garage and expected to be able to drive it on his return. It was not the newest of cars. The battery, naturally, was flat when he came to try to start it (always disconnect it if you are leaving the car for any length of time). When he tried to push start the car, he found that the brakes were jammed, and the car would not move. He eventually started the sluggish engine using jump leads connected to a friend's car. He found that the engine stalled when he tried to drive it, because of the problem with the brakes. Revving the engine hard, he let out the clutch. The brakes freed with a loud bang, and the car moved with a ripping sound as the tyres, which had begun to decompose, left chunks of tread on the garage floor.

DO YOU INTEND TO RETURN?

There is no simple advice to give. If you are not intending to return, it makes sense to sell up and move permanently. If you find this hard, you should ask yourself whether you really do want to go at all. If you are intending the stay to be relatively short, then find a tenant. However, you may still have problems even if you use a letting agent. The best tenants are companies or governments who want to find long-term housing for their seconded staff. Then you are unlikely to have the sorts of problems which I have described.

GETTING ACCOMMODATION ABROAD

Accommodation abroad is also potentially a problem. If you are lucky, the employer will arrange all this for you. However, there have been cases where employers have set people up in expensive hotels to start with, and then done nothing to help them find a more permanent place. The result has been that most of the extra money earned on the assignment has been lost in rent. If your employer is finding you a place to live in, make sure that it is signed and sealed before making your move. If he or she has only found you temporary shelter, get written assurance that he or she will help you to find a more permanent, and cheaper, place in due course.

None of this can help with an unscrupulous employer. A consultant was offered a job in the Middle East. He knew that the company had some difficulties, but was assured that it was quite safe for him to move his whole family out there; nothing would go wrong. As soon as he moved, the company went bankrupt - they had actually known before he even started that this would happen. He was stuck in a foreign country with none of the safety nets you would expect. He made the best of it, found another job, and stayed long enough to benefit from the move. Nevertheless, the affair was very worrying at the time and he would be reluctant to repeat the experience.

TAKING YOUR BELONGINGS WITH YOU

Whether or not you are moving into unfurnished accommodation, you will want to transport some of your belongings over with you. This can be quite an expensive exercise, and also time consuming. There are specialist companies which deal with this kind of removal. Your *Yellow Pages* will be the best source for this or the embassy of your destination country (*see* Appendices I and II).

What typically happens is that the remover puts your belongings into a container, which then travels by sea to your destination. The problem is that you will be parted from your belongings for a minimum of around six weeks - and more likely for much longer. Apart from the transit time, there are always customs delays. Unfortunately nobody can guarantee exactly when the things will arrive - they can only make an educated guess. Make sure, therefore, that you do not pack anything which you will need as soon as you arrive. This is much harder than it sounds. If you are going to an unfurnished house or apartment, even the most mundane item (such as a saucepan) will be needed when you arrive. For this reason, you may well need to stay in a hotel or furnished place until your goods arrive.

It is most likely that your overseas appointment will be organised either through a UK-based agent, or the company employing you. In this case, most of the details will probably be taken into account for you. Make sure, however, that no assumptions - particularly in regard to the time you may need in temporary furnished accommodation - are made which rely on third parties delivering on time. If you are contractually bound after six weeks to go into an unfurnished house or apartment, because that is the time it takes to deliver your own belongings, you may have to buy duplicate items to replace your own before they are delivered late.

PROBLEMS WITH PETS

There is also a potential problem with pets. The UK seems unique in its quarantine arrangements. Therefore you should not have a problem moving an animal abroad in most cases. However, think about how a pet, used to a temperate climate, will respond to a drastic change (to the tropics, for instance). It may be very cruel to subject it to that - it may be better to find a home for it in England before you leave.

Think too about your return. If you take your beloved moggie away with you and then come back in nine months, the cat will have to spend six more months in quarantine before returning to you. Therefore, if your stay is going to be relatively short, leave the pet behind.

WHAT GOODS TO TAKE?

You should also think carefully about the non-material goods which you are taking. For instance, is it worth the cost of transporting a car, when a local purchase can be far cheaper? There are some countries, such as Australia, where the tax on cars is so high that you should not contemplate going without one. Although the rules are tougher now, many Australians working over here used to buy extremely expensive Jaguars, Mercedes and Porsches which they could sell, even used, for double what they had paid when they returned home.

Electronic and electrical goods can be a problem. What is the local voltage? Mains powered goods from England run on 230 volts; the American norm is 110. You cannot use them over there without a transformer - and heavy 'white' goods are useless over there because the transformer would be too large to drive them.

Televisions and video-recorders cause a problem. We use a 'PAL', 625 line, 50 frames per second system here. This is common to a lot of Europe (but not France). In New Zealand, South Africa and Australia they use a slightly different system and your products need to be converted to this system. In America the system is completely different ('NTSC', 525 line and 60 frames per second). It would be pointless to take English televisions and video-recorders there.

Even such things as hi-fi equipment and computers can be a problem. You may think that one amplifier is just like the other but different standards apply to different markets. For instance, the transformers in UK products are different from those in US products. This is not just to cater for the different voltages, but also for the different frequency (50 Hz in Europe, 60 Hz in the USA). Because of the effect of hysteresis (in simple terms magnetic 'resistance'), European transformers will run hotter if used on a different mains frequency. This will potentially reduce the life of your equipment, unless the capability was actually designed for from the start.

All these little details will need to be taken into account - quite apart from the differences in customs and the natural unsettling of your routine. As long as you realise that they are there, you should be able to handle them. But remember that there will be many other problems which you cannot possibly foresee.

CHAPTER 11

UK TAXATION OF OVERSEAS EARNINGS

I once knew a man who claimed never to pay any tax. He worked in one country after another, had more than one passport (legitimately), and the tax authorities never caught up with him. Unfortunately this will not apply to many of us.

Taxation of overseas earnings can be a rather complex business, beyond the scope of a normal UK accountant. It is essential to find an expert in the field who can guide you through the potential minefield before you start. If you are using an agency to find your job, they will almost certainly be able to recommend someone suitable - or will have someone attached to the agency who can guide you in the matter.

TAX ON YOUR EARNINGS

Earnings abroad, kept abroad, will only be subject to tax in the UK if you stay away for more than one tax year, and if the country in which you work has not actually taxed the money. Of course, if you are not intending to come home, you will merely be subject (after the expiry of the tax year in which you make the move) to whatever local taxes apply.

Similarly, if you stay away over a whole tax year, you are unlikely to be asked to pay any tax in the UK for that year when you finally return. Unfortunately, these matters can be rather complex and, to some extent, up to the discretion of a tax inspector. That is why you need an accountant, who will know how to present your case.

TAX ON OVERSEAS RESIDENTS

There is a problem in establishing that you have actually settled abroad. Naturally, if you sell up and move permanently overseas, and never return, there is no question that you are no longer resident in the UK. However, if you make visits here - particularly business-related - or you keep a house or flat (perhaps renting it out), then it could be argued that you are still at least partially resident in this country. In that case, it will be necessary to convince your taxman, either personally or through your accountant, that you are indeed no longer resident in this country.

In general terms, you should be able to maintain non-resident status if you stay out of the country for more than six months in any one year, and three months on average over three years, and are paid overseas.

If you officially cease to be resident in the UK during a tax year, you gain some important benefits. The first is that you can now pro-rate any tax already paid on PAYE to gain a rebate. The way this works is that PAYE is actually calculated not on your periodic earnings, but on their pro-rated value over a year. For instance, if you earn £1,500 in a month, and have tax free pay via your tax coding of £4,000 per year, the tax for the month will be based on the notional pro-rated value of your earnings so far, less the tax allowance - £18,000 minus £4000 equals £14,000. The yearly tax on that sum will be calculated, and then pro-rated back down to a monthly figure - the amount payable would then be the difference between this figure and what you paid in the year up to that point. This pro-rating system is quite effective in taking into account periodic fluctuations in earnings, and explains why, if you get a raise in the early months of the tax year, you are initially more heavily taxed than you would expect.

If you become resident overseas during a tax year, you cease to be due to pay tax in the UK in that year, but your allowance remains in force. As a result you will probably have actually paid too much tax, and can obtain a rebate.

A second benefit of overseas resident status is that you will not be liable to capital gains tax in the UK. If you invest and realise a capital gain while you are abroad, you will not be liable to UK tax. Of course, if you are back in the UK when you realise the gain you will be taxed.

Many countries have 'double taxation' arrangements with the UK. What this means is not that you are taxed twice, but that the tax on overseas earnings is paid overseas, and that any UK earnings are taxed in this country - in other words you only pay tax when and where you happen to be at the time.

RETURNING TO THE UK

It is when or if you decide to return to the UK permanently that the fun can start. If this is within a short time (perhaps you decide you do not like the overseas life), you are liable to find that your money earned overseas will all be taxable - particularly if it was paid tax-free (in the Middle East, for instance). If you return after a good period, you will not have a problem except on earnings in the year in which you return, if you re-patriate them. Both cases are going to be open to interpretation, and you must obtain professional advice on how best to cope with them.

In short, the taxation of foreign earnings can be quite complex and involved. However, the Inland Revenue are already very over-stretched, and will probably treat you well if you can show that you have used a professional adviser to present your case in a concise way to them which fits in with their requirements. Conversely they will probably spend a lot of effort in getting to the bottom of your affairs if you try to pull the wool over their eyes.

APPENDIX I

A SAMPLE QUESTIONNAIRE FOR EMBASSIES

This form is a list of questions which you should ask before moving to your chosen country. It is assumed that you have already made your choice, and found a post in the country. It is not comprehensive, and you will certainly find other questions which you will want to add to it.

- Often the embassy will respond with a standard printed brochure covering the salient points which you will need to know.

- What is the normal rate of income taxation, and of sales/value added taxation?

- Is housing readily available for rent? For purchase?

- Is a work permit required for British citizens?

- If so, what is the procedure for obtaining such a permit?

- Are there restrictions on the purchase of property by foreign nationals?

- Are there restrictions on changing jobs, or locations of jobs by foreign nationals?

- Please indicate restrictions on driving by foreign nationals.

- Please indicate any special medical entry requirements (such as innoculations recommended).

- Please describe your requirements for naturalisation of foreign nationals.

- Please describe any restrictions on the export of money earned in your country.

- Are there exit requirements from your country by foreign nationals?

APPENDIX II

EMBASSY ADDRESSES

Australian High Commission
Australia House
The Strand
London
WC2B 4LA

☎ (071) 379 4334

Embassy of the Republic of Austria
18 Belgrave Mews West
London
SW1X 8HU

☎ (071) 235 3731

The Embassy of the State of Bahrain
98 Gloucester Road
London
SW7 4AU

☎ (071) 370 5132/3

The Belgian Embassy
103 Eaton Square
London
SW1W 9AB

☎ (071) 235 5422

The Canadian High Commission
Macdonald House
1 Grosvenor Square
London
W1X 0AB

☎ (071) 629 9492

The Danish Embassy
55 Sloane Street
London
SW1X 9SR

☎ (071) 235 1255

Embassy of the Arab Republic of Egypt
26 South Street
London
W1Y 9DE

☎ (071) 499 2401

The French Embassy
58 Knightsbridge
London
SW1X 7JT

☎ (071) 235 8080

The Embassy of the Federal Republic of Germany
23 Belgrave Square
London
SW1X 8PZ

☎ (071) 235 5033

The Greek Embassy
1a Holland Park
London
W11 3TP

☎ (071) 727 8040

Hong Kong Government Office
6 Grafton Street
London
W1X 3LB

☎ (071) 499 9821

The Italian Consulate
38 Eaton Place
London
SW1

☎ (071) 235 9371

Embassy of Japan
46 Grosvenor Street
London
W1X 0BA

☎ (071) 493 6030

The Kenyan High Commission
24/25 New Bond Street
London
W1Y 9HD

☎ (071) 636 2371

High Commission for the Federation of Malaysia
45 Belgrave Square
London
SW1X 8QT

☎ (071) 235 8033

The Netherlands Embassy
38 Hyde Park Gate
London
SW7 5DP

☎ (071) 584 5040 or 071 581 3458

New Zealand High Commission
New Zealand House
80 Haymarket
SW1Y 4TQ

☎ (071) 930 8422

High Commission for the Federal Republic of Nigeria
Nigeria House
9 Northumberland Avenue
London
WC2N 5BX

☎ (071) 839 1244

The Norwegian Embassy
25 Belgrave Square
London
SW1X 8QD

☎ (071) 235 7151

The Portuguese Embassy
11 Belgrave Square
London
SW1X 8PP

☎ (071) 235 5331

The Royal Embassy of Saudi Arabia
30 Belgrave Square
London
SW1X 8QB

☎ (071) 235 0831

High Commission for the Republic of Singapore
9 Wilton Crescent
London
SW1X 8FA

☎ (071) 235 8315/8

Embassy of the Republic of South Africa
South Africa House
Trafalgar Square
London
WC2N 5DP

☎ (071) 930 4488

Embassy of the Kingdom of Spain
24 Belgrave Square
London
SW1X 8QA

☎ (071) 235 5555

The Royal Swedish Embassy
11 Montagu Place
London
W1H 2AL

☎ (071) 724 2101

Embassy of the Swiss Confederation
16/18 Montagu Place
London
W1H 2BQ

☎ (071) 723 0701

The Embassy of the United Arab Emirates
30 Princes Gate
London
SW7 1PT

☎ (071) 581 1281

The Embassy of the United States of America
24 Grosvenor Square
London
W1A 1AE

☎ Tel: (071) 499 9000

APPENDIX III

EUROPEAN COMPUTING SERVICES ASSOCIATIONS

AUSTRIA:

Verband Osterreichischer Software Industrie
c/o Dataservice
Landstrasse Haupstr. 5
1030 Vienna

☎ 43222 71143265
Contact: Mr Kurt Dolinek

BELGIUM:

Insea Rue des Drapiers 21
1050 Brussels

☎ 322 510 2311 or 322 510 2541
Contact: Mr Marcel Lengeler

DENMARK:

ESF EDB Systemleverandorernes
Forening
Amdmiralgade 15
DK 1066 Copenhagen K

☎ 45 33 93 16 60
Contact: Mr Finn Martin Jensen

FRANCE:

Syntec Informatique
3 Rue Leon Bonnat
75016 Paris

☎ 331 4524 43 53
Contacts: Pierre Dellus / Jean Claude Corniou

GERMANY:

Bundesverband Deutscher
Unternehmensberater (BDU)
Friedrich-Wilhelm Strasse 2
5300 Bonn 1

☎ 49228 238055/6/7/8
Contact: Mr Jurgen Ropertz

ITALY:

Associazione Nazionale Aziende Servize Informatica e
    Telematica (ANASIN)
Via Santa Tecla 4
20122 Milano

☎ 392 870768 / 862134
Contact: Mr Italo Neri

NETHERLANDS:

Vereniging Computer Service & Software Bureaus (COSSO)
Koningin Julianaplein 30-06B
Kantorencentrum 'Babylon'
Postbus 11760
'S-Gravenhage

☎ 3170 383 57 01
Contact: Dr John Borking

NORWAY:

Norske Databedrifters Landsforbund
PO Box 1632 Vika
0119 Oslo 1

☎ 472 83 89 70
Contact: Mr Hans Paulsen

PORTUGAL:

Accociaco Portuguesa das Empresas de Servicios de
    Informatica (APESI)
Rua Tenente Espanca 34
1000 Lisboa

☎ 3511 793 91 68
Contact: Mr Jose Paulo Santos

SPAIN:

Associacion Espanola Empresas Informatica (SEDISI)
Diagonal 618 3 A
08021 Barcelona

☎ 343 209 9022
Contact: Mr Florenci Bach

SWEDEN:

Dataserviceforegetagens Branschorganisation (SEBRO)
Box 4049
S-102 61 Stockholm

☎ 468 42 24 50
Contact: Mr Lennart Ring

SWITZERLAND:

SWICO (Swiss Association of the Information Community
    and Organisation Industry)
Badenerstrasse 356
c/o Computer AG
CH 8040 Zurich

☎ 411 492 4848
Contact: Dr Kurt S Muller (President)

UNITED KINGDOM:

Computing Services Association (CSA)
Hanover House
73/74 High Holborn
London WC1V 6LE

☎ 071 405 2171
Contact: Dr Doug Eyeions

APPENDIX IV

COMPARATIVE PAY FIGURES

	Pre Tax	Post Tax	Buying Power
UK	20,000	15,000	15,000
France	30,000	23,000	20,000
Germany	40,000	25,500	21,000
Italy	31,000	20,500	18,500
Belgium	32,000	18,000	15,700
Holland	31,000	18,000	16,000
Greece	14,000	9,000	11,500
Spain	24,500	17,000	16,500
Denmark	30,000	14,000	10,500
Norway	26,000	17,000	12,500
Sweden	23,000	12,000	8,750
South Africa	17,000	12,000	15,500
Australia	21,000	13,500	15,500
New Zealand	19,500	13,500	15,000
Canada	27,000	18,000	20,000
USA	36,000	24,000	23,500

Enter Europe
via
the Riverbank

APPENDIX V

A LIST OF AGENCIES

KEY: Number of Contractors Out - A=1-10, B=11-20, C=21-40, D=41-70, E=71-100, F=101-150, G=150-200, H=201-300, I=301-400, J=400+

ABRAXAS COMPUTER SERVICES LTD 357 Euston Road, London NW1 3AL **Tel:** (071) 388 2061 **Fax:**071-387 3699 **Est:** 1974 **Directors:** R. Hill, R. Merrigan, P. Vey, R. Crawford, S. Jessop **Nos:** UK:H, Europe:D, USA:D **Regions:** South East/West London, Home Counties, Midlands, North West/East **Countries:**Benelux Countries, Germany, France, Italy, Spain, Scandinavia, USA **Staff Used:** Progs, Analyst Progs, Analysts, Project Managers, Systems Progs, Tech Support, Software Engineers, Hardware Engineers, Engineers, Operators Machine Types: IBM, ICL, DEC/VAX, Prime, Unisys, Bull, HP, NCR, Tandem, Wang, IBM compatible pc **Areas of Specialisation:** Banking & Finance, Manufacturing, Defence, Communications, Public Sector, Retail & Distribution **Company Offers:**Help with Limited Company Formation, Guide for First-Timers, Personal Accident/Sickness, Financial Advice **Payment Details:** Weekly or Monthly by BACS.

One of the largest and longest established recruitment businesses in the UK, providing comprehensive cover of all major contracts markets in the UK, also growing opportunities for contract and permanent positions in Europe and USA.

COMPUTER PEOPLE INTERNATIONAL Victory House, 7 Selsdon Way, City Harbour, London, E14 9GL **Tel**: (071) 510 2000 **Contact** Charmaine McMillan **Parent Co.:** Computer People Group plc **Directors:** M J Bayfield, R Berman (US), A J Cross, A G Lambie, J R Pinder, A C Vickers **Est:** 1974 **Nos:** USA Japan: J **Countries:**USA, Japan, Europe Staff Used: Progs, Analyst Progs, Analysts, Project Managers, System Progs, Software Engineers, Business Consultants, Tech Support, Operations, Networking, Communications, DBA **Programming Skills:** All **Operating Skills:** IBM all UNIX. Unisys, DEC, various **DBMS Skills:** DB2, IDMS, Oracle, Adabus, DL1, IMS, Ingres, DBase, various **Machine Types:** IBM, ICL, Digital, Unisys, Tandem, various **Area of Specialisation:** Banking & Finance, Manufacturing, Defence, Communications, Public Sector, Retail & Distribution **Company Offers:** Personal Accident/ Sickness Cover, Insurance Policies, Relocation Package including flights and visa costs **Payment Details:**Semi-monthly, ADP. Computer People Group is the UK's largest international computer staffing consultancy with 17 years of experience in relocation especially to its 12 US offices. Consultants have the assurance of knowing Computer People International is part of a public company, financially secure and stable. Contact our office for details of our comprehensive relocation and benefits packages - (071) 836 8411. *For further details see the inside front cover of this book.*

EUROLINK GROUP PLC Blenheim House, 56 Old Steine, Brighton BN1 1NH **Tel:** (0273) 202316 **Fax:**(0273) 205614 **Contact:** Tim Giles **Est:** 1979 **Directors:**A. G. Antoniades (Chairman), R. Kinloch (M.D.), D. Wood **Nos:**UK:J, Europe:C, USA:F, Australia/NZ:E **Regions:** Nationwide offices in Brighton, Southampton, Swindon, Central London, Manchester, Edinburgh **Countries:** USA, Australia, Europe **Staff Used:** Progs, Analyst Progs, Analysts, Project Managers, System Progs, Tech Support, Software Engineers **Machine Types:** IBM, ICL, DEC/VAX,, Prime, Unisys, IBM AS400, IBM Compatible PC **Area of Specialisation:** Banking & Finance, Public Sector, Retail, Insurance, Building Society **Company Offers:** Help with Limited Company Formation, Guide for First-Timers, Training Courses **Payment Details:** Monthly. Significant proportion of Business is in the Software Development and Applications Support area for major corporations throughout the UK. Specialists in project work in building society and banking environments.

DUX INTERNATIONAL LTD Riverbank House, Putney Bridge Approach, London, SW6 3JD **Tel:** (071) 371 9191. *For more details see p. 202 of this book.*

HOWARD ORGANISATION 24/26 Boulton Road, Stevenage, Herts SG1 4QX **Tel:** 0438 746600 **Fax:** 0438 728318. *For further details see page 170 of this book.*

HUNTERSKIL INTERNATIONAL Project House, 110-113 Tottenham Court Road, London W1P 9HG **Tel:** +44

71 383 3888 **Fax:** +44 71 387 2048. *For further details see page 120 of this book.*

IBS CONSULTING SERVICES LTD 45 Sackville Gardens, Hove, Sussex BN3 4GL **Tel:** 0273 730 982 (24 hour), 0273 730 914.

INTERNATIONAL SOLUTIONS Novogate, London W1A 4RH **Tel:** 071-487 3493 **Contact:** Michael Marks BSc (Econ) A.C.A., M.O.I. **Area of Specialisation:** International Tax and Financial Consultancy **Company Offers:** Comprehensive commercial, fiscal and tax packages for contracts in Germany, Belgium, France, Spain, Switzerland and other European and Scandinavian countries. Integrated services provided by professionally qualified and experienced consultants. Consultations and continued assistance throughout term of overseas assignments and beyond.

INTERSKILL SERVICES Crown House, Manchester Road, Wilmslow, SK9 1BH **Tel:** 0625 539669 **Fax:** 0625 535566 **Contact:** Andy Johnston. **Directors:** Jim Shaw. **Nos:** UK: J. Europe: E. **Regions:** All regions **Countries:** Throughout Europe and US **Staff Used:** Progs, Analyst Progs, Systems Analysts, Business Analysts, Project Managers, Systems Progs, Software Engineers, Tech Support, PC Support, Operations Analysts, Operations, Networking, Communications, DBA, Technical Authors **Programming Skills:** Cobol, 4GL, RPG3, PL/1, C, Basic, RPG2, Quickbuild, Assembler **Operating Skills:** IBM AS/400, IBM MVS, ICL VME, IBM System 38, Unix, DEC VAX VMS, IBM System 36, MS-DOS, IBM DOS/VSE **DBMS Skills:** DB2, IDMS, Oracle, Adabas, DL1, IMS, DBase **Machine Type:** IBM, ICL, Digital, Prime, Unisys, Bull, HP, Tandem, Wang **Area of Specialisation:** Banking & Finance, Manufacturing, Communications, Public Sector, Retail &

Distribution **Company Offers:** Help with Limited Company Formation Service plus practical help on working on the Continent **Payment Details:** Monthly, Percentage divulged, Monthly by cheque in the UK & by International Banking Transfer on the Continent. We specialise in providing senior and specialist DP professionals of all disciplines to blue-chip companies throughout Europe, (including the UK) and offer a tax efficient and above board employment package to our consultants working on the Continent. We pay our contractors 80% of client billings for normal hours worked and 95% of overtime.

JCC LIMITED 106 London Road, St. Albans, Hertfordshire AL1 1NX **Tel:** (0727) 836361 **Fax:** (0727) 860033 **Contact:** Siobhan O'Kelly **Est:** 1986 **Directors:** A. G. Cotton **Nos:** UK:E **Staff Used:** Progs, Analyst Progs, Analysts, System Progs, Tech Support, Software Engineers, Hardware Engineers, Systems Managers, Operators

JCC B.V. Schorpioenstraat 282, 3067 KW Rotterdam, 3009 CA Rotterdam, Nederland **Tel:** (010 31) 10 456155 **Fax:** (010 31) 10 4565528 **Contact:** David Clayden **Est:** 1981 **Directors:** A. G. Cotton **Nos:** O/Seas:E **Countries:**Holland, Belgium, Luxembourg, France **Staff Used:**Progs, Analyst Progs, Analysts, System Progs, Tech Support, Software Engineers, Hardware Engineers, Systems Managers.

JCC GmbH Baumgarten 5, 6200 Wiesbaden, Bundesrepublik, Deutschland **Tel:** (010 49) 611 701021 **Fax:** (010 49) 611714046 **Contact:** Dick Kuster **Est:** 1989 **Directors:** A. G. Cotton **Nos:** O/Seas:E **Countries:**Germany, Australia **Staff Used:** Progs, Analyst Progs, Analysts, System Progs, Tech Support, Software Engineers, Hardware Engineers, Systems Managers, Operators.

JOHN STEPHEN ACCOUNTANCY SERVICE *See under S later in this list.*

KNIGHT PROGRAMMING SUPPORT Premier House, 1 Canning Street, Harrow, Middlesex HA3 7TS **Tel:** 081 863 0049 **Fax:** 081 861 3245. *For further details see page 176 of this book.*

PEOPLE IN COMPUTERS LIMITED Iron Bridge House, 3 Bridge Approach, London NW1 8BD **Tel:** (071) 722 5808 **Fax:** 071-586 1217 **Contact:** Geoff Price **Parent:** People in Computers Pty Limited **Est:** 1982 **Directors:** Geoff Price, Brian Newbert, Joe Marshall **Nos:** UK/Australia:G **Regions:** Throughout the UK **Staff Used:** Progs, Analyst Progs, Systems Analysts, Project Managers, Systems Progs, DBA, Tech Support, PC Support **Machine Types:** IBM, Digital, Bull, HP, Tandem, IBM/Compatible PC **Area of Specialisation:** Insurance, Oil, Motor, Public Sector, Retail & Distribution, Banking & Finance **Company Offers:** Help with Limited Company Formation, Guide for First-Timers **Payment Details:** Fortnightly. Australia's Leading independent contracting house with branches in Melbourne, Sydney and Perth. Our London office is now expanding rapidly and we are always looking for quality people for the UK and Australia.

REAL TIME CONSULTANTS LTD 118-120 Warwick Street, Leamington Spa, Warwickshire CV32 4QY **Tel:**(0926) 313133 **Fax:** (0926) 422165 **Contact:** C. Nugent **Est:** 1980 **Nos:** F **Countries:** UK, Holland, Germany, France, Belgium **Staff Used:** Progs, Analyst Progs, Systems Analysts, Business Analysts, Project Managers, System Progs, Software Engineers, Tech Support, Networking, Communications, DBA **Programming Skills:** ADA, C, Assembler, RTL/2, PASCAL, Fortran, Coral, Powerhouse **Operating Skills:** Unix, DEC VAX VMS, MS-DOS, RSX DBMS Skills: Oracle, Ingres, Empress **Machine Types:** Digital, Intel, Motorola, Sun, Prime, Unisys, Bull, HP, Tandem **Areas of Specialisation:** Manufacturing, Defence, Communications, Banking & Finance **Company Offers:**Training courses **Payment Details:** Monthly. Specialists in real-time, technical and scientific sector of the market throughout the UK and Europe. Preferred suppliers to major clients within areas such as Military and Defence, Telecommunications, Manufacturing and Industrial. We offer contracting, consultancy, support and fixed-priced projects. For the contractor we have an excellent track record in providing follow-on contracts in addition to all the benefits of dealing with a highly reputable company that has been established for over 10 years.

SOFTWARE 92 PLC 7 Trinity Place, Midland Drive, Sutton Coldfield, B72 1TX **Tel:** (021) 354 9911 *For further details see page 8 of this book.*

SHUTER SMITH INTERNATIONAL Harrier House, St Albans Road East, Hatfield, Herts AL10 0HE **Tel:**0707 272911 **Fax:** 0707 260122. *For further details see the inside back cover of this book.*

John Stephen Accountancy Services

JOHN STEPHEN ACCOUNTANCY SERVICE - JSA - offer the complete range of accounting services including Company Formations - both 'on' and 'off' shore - Accounts Preparation and Year End Audit; monthly Payroll & PAYE etc; quarterly Dividends and VAT; as well as a complete range of Financial Services. However, what makes them unique is that they only accept one type of client - the Limited Company Contractor. With such a specialised client base, their experience with overseas contracts and contractors is probably unrivalled in the UK today! They offer under one roof a degree of service and specialisation second to none. And all this for one low cost, FIXED fee. Call (071) 355 4569 or (081) 903 6030 for a FREE, no obligation appointment at either their central London or Wembley office.

INDEX

COMPUTER WEEKLY PUBLICATIONS

Computer Weekly is the UK's leading weekly computer newspaper which goes to over 112,000 computer professionals each week. Founded in 1967, the paper covers news, reviews and features for the computer industry. In addition, *Computer Weekly* also publishes books relevant to and of interest to its readership.

Publications to date (obtainable through your bookshop or by ringing (081) 661 3099/3050) are:

COMPUTER WEEKLY GUIDE TO 300 KEY IT COMPANIES

This up-to-date, independent, analytical guide to 300 key software and hardware suppliers has been compiled to meet the demand for independent information about individual companies, which is here brought together in a highly accessible form.

The 300 companies have been selected according to a number of criteria. These include: the impact of the company within the UK, the degree of production within the UK, and the size of the company.

The late Keith Jones, who wrote about the hardware companies, was formerly European Editor of the US magazine *Mini-Micro Systems*. Phil Manchester, who has covered the software companies, was formerly Editor of the *Financial Times Fintech Software Newsletter*.

ISBN 1-85384-026-2   304 pages   A4 size   Price £65

ALIENS' GUIDE TO THE COMPUTER INDUSTRY
by John Kavanagh

In a lucid and light style, leading computer industry writer John Kavanagh discusses how the various parts of the computer industry inter-relate and what makes it tick. Complete with extensive index, the book is invaluable for all who come into contact with the computer industry.

'Business professionals who worry about their grasp of the general computing scene and do not want to be bombarded with jargon and technicalities, will get good value ... an excellent 'snapshot' of the companies, the current areas of interest and the problems' *Financial Times*

ISBN 1-85384-012-2   192 pages   A5 size   Price £9.95

COMPUTER JARGON EXPLAINED
by Nicholas Enticknap

Following reader demand this is a totally revised, expanded and updated version of our highly successful guide to computer jargon, *Breaking the Jargon*.

This 176 page book provides the context to and discusses 68 of the most commonly used computer jargon terms. Extensively cross-indexed this book is essential reading for all computer professionals, and will be useful to many business people too.

'... a useful shield against the constant barrage of impossible language the computer business throws out' *The Independent*

'... a worthwhile investment' *Motor Transport*

ISBN 1-85384-015-7   176 pages   A5 size   Price £9.95

WHAT TO DO WHEN A MICRO LANDS ON YOUR DESK
by Glyn Moody and Manek Dubash

This book will help you get the most out of your microcomputer. It is a practical book, giving advice on how to make the transition from typewriter to micro profitably and with minimum effort.

The authors look at software - wordprocessing, databases, spreadsheets, graphics and communications - and the different types of hardware on the market. The book contains valuable information on training, health and security, and legal matters including the Data Protection Act, operating systems, the history of the computer, the current micro scene and the future.

ISBN 1-85384-011-4   296 pages   A5 size   Price £14.95

CONSIDERING COMPUTER CONTRACTING?
by Michael Powell

This is a completely revised and updated edition of the highly successful book which has helped many computer professionals break loose from being employees to working freelance, in some cases doubling their salaries.

There is information on: who uses computer contractors and why; what it takes to become a contract worker; how to find your first contract; how to keep your skills updated; forming your own company and handling finances; contract agencies.

ISBN 1-85384-022-X   176 pages   A5 size   Price £12.95

HITCHHIKERS' GUIDE TO ELECTRONICS IN THE '90S
by David Manners

Developments in electronics underpin not only the computer industry but also the whole of modern society. This book is essential if DP and IT professionals are to identify trends that will affect all our jobs in the 1990s.

David Manners, an awarding winning senior editor on *Electronics Weekly* newspaper, lucidly explains the electronics industry and its key products and discusses its central role and implications to industry in the 1990s.

Essential reading for IT staff, marketing and sales directors, strategic planners and all interested in the future of the IT industry.

ISBN 1-85384-020-3   224 pages   A5 size   Price £12.95

A SIMPLE INTRODUCTION TO DATA AND ACTIVITY ANALYSIS
by Rosemary Rock-Evans

Successful analysis of business operations is a prerequisite to building any computer system within a company. Whereas many existing books approach this topic from an academic point of view, this is the fruit of years of practical analysis in blue chip companies.

Rosemary Rock-Evans is a leading consultant. Her first book on this topic for *Computer Weekly*, published in 1981, is now out of print. However, the considerable demand within the industry for this book has resulted in this totally revised and updated version.

It is essential reading for all analysts in the computer industry, and is also recommended for students to give them a taste of the real world of analysis.

ISBN 1-85384-001-7   272 pages   A4 size   Price £24.95

OPEN SYSTEMS: THE BASIC GUIDE TO OSI
AND ITS IMPLEMENTATION
by Peter Judge

We recognise the need for a concise, clear guide to the complex area of computer standards, untrammelled by jargon and with appropriate and comprehensible analogies to simplify this difficult topic.

This book, a unique collaboration between *Computer Weekly* and the magazine *Systems International*, steers an independent and neutral path through this contentious area and is essential for users and suppliers. It is required reading for all who come into contact with the computer industry.

ISBN 1-85384-009-2   192 pages   A5 size   Price £12.95

IT PERSPECTIVES CONFERENCE: THE FUTURE OF THE IT INDUSTRY

Many nuggets of strategic thought are contained in this carefully edited transcript of the actual words spoken by leading IT industry decision makers at *Computer Weekly*'s landmark conference held late in 1987.

The conference was dedicated to discussing current and future directions the industry is taking from four perspectives: supplier perspectives; communications perspectives; user perspectives and future perspectives.

'... makes compelling reading for those involved in the business computer industry' *The Guardian*

'... thought-provoking points and some nice questions put to speakers at the end' *Daily Telegraph*

ISBN 1-85384-008-4   224 pages   A4 size   Price £19.95

COMPUTER WEEKLY BOOK OF PUZZLERS
Compiled by Jim Howson

Test your powers of lateral thinking with this compendium of 187 of the best puzzles published over the years in *Computer Weekly*. The detailed explanations of how solutions are reached make this a useful guide to recreational mathematics. No computer is needed to solve these fascinating puzzles.

'... a pleasant collection of puzzles exercises for computer freaks. Actually probably fewer than half the puzzles here need a computer solution ...' *Laboratory Equipment Digest*

ISBN 1-85384-002-5   160 pages   A5 size   Price £6.95

WOMEN IN COMPUTING
by Judith Morris

Written by a respected former editor of several computer magazines, this book reflects the upsurge in awareness of the important role women can play in helping to stem the critical skills shortage within the computer industry.

The book addresses women's issues in a practical and sensible way and is aimed at all business women both in the computer industry or who work with computers. Contains much practical advice, including the names and addresses of useful organisations, and a valuable further reading list.

ISBN 1-85384-004-1   128 pages   A5 size   Price £9.95

HOW TO GET JOBS IN MICROCOMPUTING
by John F Charles

As micros proliferate, opportunities for getting jobs in this area are expanding rapidly. The author, who has worked with micros in major organisations, discusses how to get started in microcomputing, describes the different types of job available, and offers tips and hints based on practical experience.

ISBN 1-85384-010-6   160 pages   A5 size   Price £6.95

LOW COST PC NETWORKING
by Mike James

The whole area of PC networking is taking off rapidly now. Can you afford to be left behind? Mike James' book shows how networking revolutionises the way we use PCs and the tasks that they perform. It also explains how networking goes further than simply linking PCs, and how it enables you to integrate your operations to transform your business.

Chapters cover every aspect of networking, from planning your network and selecting the hardware and software to applications, technicalities and contacts.

ISBN 0-434-90897-5   256 pages   246 x 188 mm   Price £16.95

SELLING INFORMATION TECHNOLOGY:
A PRACTICAL CAREER GUIDE
by Eric Johnson

Selling in IT requires more skill and creativity than selling in any other profession. This handbook explains why and provides practical down-to-earth advice on achieving the necessary extra skills. A collaboration between *Computer Weekly* and the *National Computing Centre*, this book discusses career issues, general IT sales issues, and key IT industry developments.

ISBN 0-85012-684-3   244 pages   144 x 207 mm   Price £12.50

MANAGING INFORMATION SECURITY:
A NON-TECHNICAL MANAGEMENT GUIDE
by Ken Wong and Steve Watt

This book has been written by experienced consultants in what is for most people a new field. Management issues are covered in detail. Topics include: people - are they assets or liabilities, risk assessment, devising and testing a disaster recovery plan, encryption and communication security, the impact of the PC revolution, access control, combatting hacking and viruses, and security in different vertical market sectors such as banking and retail.

ISBN 0-946395-63-2   336 pages   277 x 214 mm   Price £85

BREAKDOWNS IN COMPUTER SECURITY: COMMENTARY AND ANALYSIS
by Mike Rentell and Peter Jenner

Protect yourself and your company from breaches of computer security with this jargon-free compendium and discussion of over 100 genuine incidents which took place in 1988, 1989 and 1990.

Breakdowns in security have resulted in serious, sometimes fatal, injuries, and loss of considerable sums of money, sometimes leading to bankruptcy. These incidents have involved a wide range of companies, public institutions, individuals and the state

The comment on each incident will tell you what the company concerned *should* have done to prevent or alleviate the more damaging aspects of each problem.

Breakdowns in Computer Security is essential reading for all managers who have to protect their systems against accidental and malicious destruction, interference or breach of confidentiality.

ISBN 1-85384-024-6   104 pages   A5 size   Price £12.95

COMPUTER WEEKLY GUIDE TO RESOURCES 1990

Our extensively indexed second Annual Guide fulfils the computer industry's need for an independent, handy, up-to-date reference review signposting and interpreting the key trends in the computer industry.

A key section is an indepth, independent discussion of 270 software and computer companies, invaluable for managing directors, DP managers, sales and marketing people and all executive job hunters.

Our first Annual Guide was well acclaimed:

'In spite of a plethora of guides to various aspects of the computer industry, there hasn't been one readable, comprehensive overview of the current UK scene. *Computer Weekly's* Guide to Resources has filled the bill ... it's very good.' *The Guardian*.

ISBN 1-85384-017-3   416 pages   A4 size   Price £45

THE SCANNER HANDBOOK
A Complete Guide to the Use and Applications of Desktop Scanners
by Stephen Beale and James Cavuoto

Desktop scanners are quickly becoming standard components in personal computer systems. With these electronic reading devices, you can incorporate photographs and illustrations into a desktop publishing program, convert printed documents into text files, and perform advanced-capability facsimile transmission, all from the convenience of your desktop.

The Scanner Handbook is an authoritative and informative guide to selecting, installing and using a desktop scanner. In lively and entertaining prose, the authors describe the essential features of desktop scanners and explain how best to apply scanning hardware and software.

ISBN: 0-434-90069-9   256 pages   Price £19.95

DATABASE MANAGEMENT SYSTEMS
Understanding and Applying Database Technology
by Michael M. Gorman

The next DBMS generation is here. It contains DBMSs that look alike - on the outside. This does not mean all DSMSs are the same on the inside. On the inside they perform very differently - some slow, others fast; some rudimentary, others advanced. This book is about the critical DBMS differences.

Michael Gorman goes to considerable length to detail the components of a sophisticated DBMS and to provide DBMS users and evaluators with the information they need to look critically at DBMS products. He covers batch, network and relational DBMSs that operate on mainframes, minicomputers and microcomputers.

Gorman starts with a discussion of database standards. He continues with DBMS applications and components. This includes application classification, static and dynamic relationships, DBMS components and subcomponents, and DBMS requirements. This is followed by a discussion of DBMS components - the logical database, the physical database, interrogation and system control.

Contents: ANSI Database Standards; DBMS Applications and Components; The Logical Database; The Physical Database; Interrogation; System Control; Keys and BNF Notation Definition; Glossary

ISBN: 0-7506-0135-3   480 pages   Hardback   Price: £40

THE SOFTWARE ENGINEER'S REFERENCE BOOK
Edited by John McDermid

This comprehensive and authoritative reference source covers the whole topic of software engineering, including the underlying science and mathematics, software development technology, software project management and principles of applications. It provides a thorough treatment of the science, principles and practice of software engineering, stressing fundamental and stable concepts as well as summarising the 'state of the art' in software engineering methods and tools. Offering pragmatic guidance and a sound understanding of the material covered, most chapters also contain a comprehensive set of references or a bibliography for further reading.

Produced by an internationally acclaimed team of experts from the UK, continental Europe and North America, the *Software Engineer's Reference Book* is aimed at practising software engineers, software project managers and consultants. The book is edited by John A McDermid, Professor of Software Engineering at the University of York and Director of York Software Engineering Ltd.

'The breadth of coverage is excellent...John McDermid is the ideal person to edit the book. He has the right blend of theory and pragmatism for such a project.' - Professor Darrel Ince, The Open University

Contents: Applicable mathematics; Fundamental computer science; Other relevant science and theory; Conventional development; Formal development; Software development management; AI/IKBS approaches; Other approaches to software development; Programming languages; The operational environment; Principles of application; Future developments for software engineering as a profession.

ISBN: 0-7506-1040-9   1032 pages   Hardback   Price £125

PROFITING FROM YOUR PRINTER: USERS' GUIDE TO COMPUTER PRINTING
by Frank Booty

This book will help users choose a suitable printer for their computer, and includes advice as to which manufacturer and model will meet their particular requirements. Prices of the printers are included to give an idea of pricing structures and relative costs.

Also included: how to connect a printer to your system; third/fourth party maintenance aspects; paper handling; form feeding; hidden costs; desktop publishing, and the effects of networking on printers.

ISBN 1-85384-019-X   224 pages   A5 size   Price £14.95